WOW, What a Team!

Essential Components for Successful Teaming

■●▲

by Randy Thompson and Dorothy VanderJagt

Incentive Publications, Inc.
Nashville, Tennessee

This book is dedicated to
the teachers who inspired us to start on this course,
our parents for their guidance to chart this course,
and our families for their unconditional support to keep us on this course.

Cover art by Becky Rüegger
Cover design by Marta Drayton and Joe Shibley
Illustrated by Angela Reiner
Edited by Jennifer J. Streams

Library of Congress Card Number: 00-107561
ISBN 0-86530-483-1

PRINTED IN THE UNITED STATES OF AMERICA
www.incentivepublications.com

WOW, What a Team!

■●▲

INTRODUCTION

Teaching middle school is like trying to work with Jell-O. Every time you think you have it going in the direction that you want, it starts to wiggle and move in all directions. If you try to get a hold of the Jell-O, it squirts right through your fingers. Think about this job description: wanted, someone to work with about 125 students, who are all going through puberty at the same time. Only committed (or soon to be) teachers should apply.

Middle school students have been referred to as many things, including transescant, pubescent, and even the herd of the absurd. One analogy: give or take about 20 pounds, middle school students are akin to 100-pound mosquitoes! Think about it. They fly around everywhere with no apparent destination! Just imagine trying to get a mosquito to sit still for a math lesson. A team effort is required to harness all of that early adolescent energy.

We appreciate teaming because we remember being outlaw mosquitoes in a very traditional junior high school setting. Working independently, the teachers could never quite harness and focus our energy. We were always working the teachers against each other with passes, homework, tardiness, and so on, because we knew that with the randomness of the schedule there was no way for one teacher to know what another was doing. We knew we were really in trouble when we saw two teachers talking to each other.

Early adolescence, or the middle school years, is a time of dramatic change for our youth. At no other time in their lives will they grow more socially, emotionally, physically, and intellectually than during the middle years. That is why this is such a confusing time of contradictions, challenges, and great rewards for everyone involved.

An Interdisciplinary Teaching Team (Teaming) is a way of grouping students and teachers together to eliminate the impersonal random scheduling of the junior high school. The idea is to create small communities of learning within the school. Simply defined, a middle school team is a common group of students assigned to a common group of teachers for a common part of the day.

Great middle schools have great teams. These are the teams that collaborate so well that the teachers and students create learning environments that promote high performance. When you watch these kinds of teams in action, all you can say is WOW! These teams do not work well together by accident. Teaming requires a lot of training, planning, collaboration, and follow-through.

WOW teams are productive because they make the most of their team time. The goal of this book is to look at twelve of the components of productive teams. Each chapter is designed to demonstrate a strategy that can create high impact team performance. Each chapter also includes an activity that you and your teammates may work through. The activities will help guide you and your teammates as you implement each strategy.

It is our hope that this book will provide teams with a practical guide for teaming. The stories and ideas shared here represent our personal experiences in teaching and administration in addition to a collection of the WOW strategies we have encountered in our work with teachers and students across the United States and in several other countries.

This book is designed to help experienced teams as well those just beginning to explore teaming. For novice teams, *WOW, What a Team!* will demonstrate the promise and possibilities of teaming and provide practical ideas for success as they begin the process of becoming a team. Experienced teams will find ideas and strategies to renew their purpose and take their teaming to the next level.

Middle school is sometimes referred to as "hormone heaven", and middle school teachers are definitely angels in training. Regardless of your previous experience with teaming, it is our hope that this book is helpful as your earn your wings! Enjoy!

Randy Thompson and Dorothy VanderJagt

WOW,
What a Team!

Essential Components for Successful Teaming

■●▲

TABLE OF CONTENTS

Chapter 6. Team Conferences with Students and Parents

▲ *This chapter will demonstrate how teams can get the most out of student/parent conferences with the least emotional distress.*

Chapter 7. Informative Newsletters

■ *Somewhere between the comics and the* Wall Street Journal *lies team newsletters. This chapter will teach you how to produce newsletters that will get maximum impact with minimum effort.*

Chapter 8. Flexible Scheduling

● *Do you flex your scheduling muscle? Or, does the bell often kick the sands of time in your face? This chapter will demonstrate ways for teams to really flex their schedules to maximize their instructional time.*

Chapter 9. Curriculum Development

▲ *Did the COW really jump over the moon? In this chapter we share a practical and easy way for teams to move from a departmental to an interdisciplinary style of instruction.*

Chapter 10. Professional Development

■ *Kaison is the Japanese term for continuous improvement and the daily pursuit of perfection. In this chapter you learn about professional development for teams that want to practice Kaison.*

Chapter 11. Assessing Team Success

● *This chapter has a great activity that helps you define team success, and helps you create a tool to measure how your team is doing.*

Chapter 12. Team Goals

▲ *Never have a map when you need one? In this chapter you will learn about setting team priorities and establishing team goals to give your team a road map to success.*

Chapter 1

Roles and Responsibilities of Team Members

■●▲

"What the wise do in the beginning,
fools do in the end."
—Warren Buffet

Chapter 1

Who's on first? How do you tell the players without a program? It is important that each team member knows and understands the roles and responsibilities that make for successful teaming. Each member should be willing to take on one or more of the roles, and share in the responsibility for the team's success.

The roles needed for each team should be assigned after much team discussion about the various roles and the needs of the team. Some roles, such as team leader and team recorder, are absolutely critical. Others, like team caller, are up to the particular management style the team develops.

As possible team roles and the corresponding responsibilities that accompany each role are reviewed, it becomes apparent that many of the roles can be combined. A team may also take on tasks that will generate the need for new roles unique to that team's goals. It is important that each team member take on a role to help ensure team success; however, not every team will have every role described here.

Roles should be decided on by team consensus. This is sometimes easier said than done. Roles may be assigned for various times of duration. Many teams rotate roles so that each team member has the opportunity to gain the experience of each role. For example, a four-member team may rotate roles quarterly. It is said that if you are never the lead dog, your view will always be the same. So, we want all team members to understand all of the roles and responsibilities for a team.

It is also important that all team members understand and appreciate that diversity makes for stronger teams. By diversity, we mean that the team membership should be reflective of the entire staff as much as possible. Every team should reflect the gender, ethnic, teaching experience, etc. make-up of the overall staff. Consideration should also be given to teaching and learning styles to get as many styles on each team as is possible.

Diversity on a team means that the team has a variety of talents and personalities. This is beneficial to the students as they get a variety of teaching styles and instructional strategies in their classes. Diversity is beneficial to the team members, as there are a variety of skills to complement each other. A team with diversity and shared roles and responsibilities will continue to grow and improve.

AN OUNCE OF PREVENTION

Anytime two or more people are together there is the potential for disagreement. The often quoted expression, "if two people always agree, one of them is not needed" applies well to team building. We all want to be needed, but successful teams will establish guidelines for conflict management before the "need" arises. Some of the barriers teams may have to overcome may include personality conflicts, misunderstandings, and hurt feelings. These problems are most often the result of poor communication. Teams need to anticipate potential issues and be able to apply the problem-solving skills to deal with them.

Regardless of the role, all team members must agree to support each other. WOW team members know that if they are not part of the solution, then they become part of the problem. The following list contains supportive team member behaviors that all team members must agree to exhibit.

Supportive Team Member Behaviors

▲ Engage in open and honest communication.

● Listen to understand and speak to be understood.

▲ Never be critical, negative, or manipulative.

● Participate, volunteer, and share in the responsibilities.

▲ Criticize ideas, not people, and be open-minded.

● Never use put-downs (personal attacks).

▲ Be courteous, honest, trusting, and sharing.

● Always maintain team confidentiality.

Roles and Responsibilities of Team Members

Read and reflect on the importance of the following roles and responsibilities for team members. After you have looked over the following list, we are going to give you the opportunity to pick your own team. We are going to give you the descriptions of several potential team members that are available for building a five-person team with you. To get a feel for assigning roles, you will get to choose four teachers from the list and assign the roles for your team.

As you read and consider the following roles, please note that not all teams have all of the roles listed here. Also, teams may combine roles if they feel the need for more roles than they have team members. For example, on a two-member team, one team member may be the recorder and the communicator, while the other team member might be the team leader and timekeeper.

WOW, What a Team!

Leader

The leader most often facilitates the team meetings. Leaders set the tone for meetings and therefore must be motivated and positive about teaming. They must build trust and ownership by involving everyone and encouraging open, honest communication. They generally represent the team and will act as liaison to the administration. They build team unity and may have to resolve conflict between team members.

Scribe

The scribe, also called the recorder/secretary/historian/etc., is charged with keeping the team notebook. The scribe will take notes during the team meetings, and keep any documentation determined essential to the team in the team notebook.

Timekeeper

The responsibility of the timekeeper is to keep the team on task by keeping the time for each item on the agenda. Agenda items should have a predetermined amount of time assigned them (see chapter two). The timekeeper makes the team aware of how much time is left for an item, and when it is time to move on to the next item.

Communicator

Communicators keep non-team members informed. They are to ask this question in relation to every agenda item: "Whom else do we need to inform about this?" Their next task is to inform those persons, such as the cafeteria staff, the administration, other teams, parents, etc. about team activities. This is especially helpful for remembering to communicate to the exploratory team of teachers.

Observer

Observers provide feedback to the team regarding how the team is functioning. They remind the team of accomplishments and celebrate team success. They also give feedback for any need for improvement, such as not staying on task, or other negative team or team member behaviors.

Resource Person

The responsibility of the resource person is to bring or have on hand any of the "stuff" needed for a team meeting. This might include a flip chart, the team curriculum map, the team calendar, the certificates for "Thumbs Up" meetings (see chapter five), field trip permission forms, etc.

Public Relations Person

Most often called the "PR" person, this person has the task of promoting accomplishments of the team. They will often direct putting together the team newsletter, board presentations, and media opportunities.

Other Roles

Many teams have assigned other roles as needs arise. There may be a social director to coordinate team social activities. The team caller may make all of the calls for the team (usually rotated on a weekly basis) to avoid duplication of calls. The encourager tries to make sure that everyone participates, and will encourage members as needed. Some teams will split the team leader role and create a separate facilitator role. The facilitator will run team meetings, while the team leader will perform all of the other administrative type leadership tasks.

WOW, What a Team!

Put together a five-person team by making selections from the staff members described below and including yourself as the fifth team member. Each team member has very special qualities and many of them will be familiar.

Your task is to choose team members to best complement your own talents and abilities. Remember, diversity is the key to success of a WOW team. Good luck!

The Staff Members

1. Polly Positive — Polly is the most positive person on the staff. Her glass is always half full. She does not like conflict, and will sometimes avoid issues to avoid possible conflict. She is well liked and is a real "feel good" person.

2. Robby Realistic — Robby will not make a decision without all of the "facts." He is known as a strict disciplinarian, and does not embrace change easily. He is a very left-brained thinker, so he is very well organized, and wants everything in place. He even color codes his grade book, and always has his grades in on time.

3. Carl Coach — Carl coaches three sports and while he supports teaming, he has little time to do things for the team. Because he has so little time, he often tries to grade papers and does other tasks during team time. Carl relates to the students well, and is a great motivator.

4. Karl Kissup — Karl knows everybody in a position of authority and knows who to call, and how to get anything. Karl gets things done, and is on every committee in the school. He is not the most engaging teacher, and sometimes struggles with control in his class.

5. Freda Flex — Freda is a scheduling expert. She is always playing with the schedule, and really enjoys having a different schedule every day. She does not like routine, and has little patience with those not willing to try new things right away.

6. Tom Teaming — Mr. Team player, Tom will do anything for the team. He enjoys team meetings, and will often bring food for everyone. He is not very well liked by the students because of his lecture approach to teaching. He is very traditional in his approach to teaching. He laminates his lesson plans.

7. Carla Curriculum — Carla is really into interdisciplinary units. She would have a theme for everything. A very enthusiastic teacher, she pushes very hard, and expects the other teachers to be willing to put in as much time planning as she does. Carla has no outside commitments; her teaching is her life.

8. Cathy Creative — Cathy is very creative, and very enthusiastic. She has great ideas, but lacks organizational skills. She gets things started, but has trouble with details. She is very forgetful. The students love her but get frustrated when she loses their papers.

WOW, What a Team!

9. Albert Association — Albert is the president of the Teachers Association, and is concerned about contract implications of everything under discussion. While he will not do anything "extra" without some sort of compensation, he will do anything within the contract, and is a very good teacher.

10. Connie Confidential — Connie is in the middle of everything. She has the latest scoop on all happenings going on in the school. All rumors go through Connie. She does a good job in the classroom, and really enjoys sharing the latest news at team meetings.

Who will you pick for your team? List your selections on the Team Selection Form on the following page. Also include the role or roles assigned to each, and the rationale for each choice. Start with yourself, and then add your teammates. Included on pages 21 and 22 are the authors' choices. When you have finished, you might enjoy comparing your selections with ours. There are no right or wrong answers, so have fun using creative thinking skills to build a WOW team!

Team Selection Form ━━━━━━━━━━━━━━ ■●▲

#1: <u>Yourself</u> _____ Role: _____

Rationale: _____

_____

_____

_____

#2: _____ Role: _____

Rationale: _____

_____

_____

_____

#3: _____ Role: _____

Rationale: _____

_____

_____

_____

#4: _____ Role: _____

Rationale: _____

_____

_____

_____

#5: _____ Role: _____

Rationale: _____

_____

_____

_____

WOW, What a Team!

Randy's Choices

First, we have to explain that Randy is very right-brained, which means that he is creative, but often not as organized as he would like to be. So, as much fun as it would be for him to be on a team with Cathy Creative, together they might be too great a challenge for one team. So, here are Randy's choices.

1. Yours Truly   Scribe
   - ▲ Keeping the minutes will keep my very easily-distracted personality focused.

2. Robby Realistic   Timekeeper
   - ● I know that Robby will keep us on task, which I definitely need. I also have fun frustrating those left-brainers.

3. Karl Kissup   Communicator
   - ▲ Karl will make sure our team gets what we need. As a team, we can help him with his classroom control, and it never hurts to have someone that is well-connected.

4. Carla Curriculum   Team Leader
   - ● Carla will push us. She will not let me play, and she will keep us working for the students.

5. Connie Confidential   Public Relations
   - ▲ What more can you say? She is perfect for the job. She will also keep us caught up on the latest gossip.

Honorable Mention:
- ● Freda Flex   Team Leader
  She would be able to shake things up, and keep us guessing.

- ▲ Carl Coach   Scribe
  Like me, keeping the minutes will keep him focused, and I have a soft spot for coaches.

Dorothy's Choices

Dorothy, like Randy, is also right-brained, and some of their choices may look similar. But, remember there is no "right" answer. Whatever or whoever you need to make a WOW team is the right choice for you.

1. Dorothy   Observer and Timekeeper
   - ▲ Keeping the team on task and celebrating successes or improving areas will keep me centered on the task at hand—striving toward a WOW team.

2. Carla Curriculum   Team Leader
   - ● Carla will be one step ahead of the team. She will continually stimulate new ideas and keep us centered on student learning.

3. Robby Realistic   Scribe
   - ▲ The minutes will be superb under the direction of Robby. The documentation for the team will be in order and Robby will be focused on his role.

4. Connie Confidential   Communicator
   - ● Connie will keep all of the non-team members informed of the latest happenings with the team. People seem comfortable with Connie and will listen to her direction.

5. Karl Kissup   Public Relations
   - ▲ Karl is involved in everything. He will know avenues to promote upcoming events and accomplishments. Karl keeps things moving and the team needs this positive connection.

                  WOW, What a Team!

CONCLUSION

The biggest worries that teachers have regarding teaming
are the concerns about who they might be teamed with, and
whether or not they will work well together. As you go through
the rest of this book, you will want to review your choices for
your team. Each chapter is designed to help teammates put the
WOW in teaming. Understanding the roles and responsibilities
of team members is only the beginning. Everyone involved must
understand that teaming is a process, not an event.

Henry Ford revolutionized the auto industry with teaming.
He said "Coming together is the beginning, staying together is
progress, working together is success." Once the team members'
positions are assigned, the team has to begin to work together.
Another great team player and coach, Casey Stengel, once said,
"Getting good players is easy, getting them to play good together
is the hard part." Learning how to get great team players to play
great together is how the WOW of teaming is achieved.

Chapter 2

Time Management for Teams

———————————————— ■●▲

"Doing the best at this moment puts you in the best place for the next moment."
—Oprah Winfrey

Chapter 2

Many teams complain about not getting enough done during their team meetings. Teams can be very frustrated by many time-consuming things. For example, teams often express frustration because they spend 90% of their team time talking about less than 10% of the students. Since problem students generally make up that 10%, team meetings can be very negative, and teachers do not feel very productive because they rarely have time to get into other areas such as curriculum.

Team meetings have the unfortunate potential to become a social hour with teams discussing everything except business. While an informal environment is encouraged, team meeting time is not the time to participate in Jimmy Buffett's "Coconut Telegraph" and get caught up with the local gossip. Enough work gets done in the rumor mill without dedicating team time to it.

Team meetings can include the discussion of many things. Of course, the main topic of discussion will be student issues, especially for teams in the first few years of teaming. Curriculum will become a regular topic as teams begin to integrate their curriculums. Also, there will always be the discussion of topics that fall under the heading of *administrativia.* Many things fall into this category, such as school business and paperwork. Other items that may come up in team time might include field trips, community service projects, business or community partnerships, school related issues such as upcoming events, visits by an administrator or counselor, and so on.

WOW, What a Team!

There are so many possible things teams feel the need to discuss during team meetings that it can become overwhelming at times. This is why it is so important that teams create agendas and place time limits for topics.

The sample agenda in this chapter (see Figure 2–1) demonstrates how a team might prioritize topics and assign time limits by the number of periods per topic. The form is kept simple thanks in part to the teachings of Randy's parents. Randy credits his father with his introduction to the KISS (Keep It Simple Sweetie, or Stupid; he will not share which one his father used) method of management. The team leader will facilitate the meetings according to the listed agenda items. The scribe will keep the minutes on the agenda sheet, and the team timekeeper will hold the team to the times listed. Notice the number of periods that are given to each topic and that the last period is left open. We will discuss the last period in length later, but teams should always leave the last period open.

In the sample agenda, the team allocated no more than fifteen minutes for next week's schedule. After putting together next week's schedule, the team allowed themselves ten minutes to discuss the field trip. Then they spent ten minutes each on two student issues. It is the job of the timekeeper to hold the team to these times. Notice again that the team scribe kept the minutes on the agenda form. It is not intended as a verbatim record, but rather to record the highlights of the discussion. Also, notice again that the last period is left open.

Deciding what to talk about during team time and then staying focused enough to stay on task is one of the more difficult things for teams to do. Having an agenda is only the beginning. There must be a universal law that there will always be more to do than there will be time. Therefore, teams will have to become very efficient with the use of what precious little team meeting time they have.

The object of this chapter is to demonstrate how teams can become more effective by being more efficient with their team meeting time; such as how agendas are developed, and how to maintain team focus through team meetings. Time management is critical for team success. Managing time to ensure that the team gets into topics like curriculum, in addition to the student management issues that tend to dominate team meetings, is essential.

Time Management for Teams

Read the following information about team meeting agendas, including team time management, items for discussion, and strategies for better time management. Then take the time to develop a personal sample team meeting agenda.

Team Meeting Agendas

The sample agenda that follows (Figure 2–1) is a simple example of the format for an agenda. It is important to record the date, those present, items discussed, and the result of the discussion. The agenda form provided is easy to use, and keeps teams organized with very little work.

Notice that the agenda is numbered, and that the title over the numbers is "Period." The period will designate the amount of time given to each topic. Most agendas are numbered, but the period is also a designation of time. In this case, each period represents five minutes of the team meeting time. Any time a topic is placed on the agenda, the person who put it there, or the team, will assign the number of periods that they believe they will need to discuss and come to closure on that topic. For example, if a topic is given three periods, the team feels they need fifteen minutes to deal with it.

WOW, What a Team!

SAMPLE TEAM MEETING AGENDA
AND MINUTES
Date: Thursday, October 26

Members present:

JIM	DOROTHY	WALT
RANDY	DEBRA	GEORGE

Period	Item	Discussion/Action Taken
1.	Next week's schedule	The following items were put in the team calendar.
2.		Team awards Wed., blocking Thurs. & Fri. for labs,
3.		common test Tues., writing assignment due Thurs., and a parent night reminder.
4.	Field Trip	Gave out permission forms, discussed student eligibility
5.		and chaperones. Dorothy will call parent volunteers.
6.	Johnny's behavior	It was decided that we need a team meeting with
7.		Johnny's parents. Jim will call parents.
8.	Susie's homework	Susie will continue to get an assignment sheet
9.		signed by each teacher. Her parents will sign off each night.
10.	Open	

Figure 2–1. Sample team agenda.

Teams should always leave the last period open, never pre-assigning any topics to the last five minutes. The last period is not for topics that were not completed. The last period is for setting the next meeting's agenda. If something was not finished during the current meeting, then the question becomes how much time to give to that topic at the next meeting. Do not try to finish business during the last period. Ideally, everything is finished during the team meeting, and the last period will be a cushion between team time, and getting back to class.

By determining how much time to give each topic, a team will not try to put more on an agenda than they can handle. If a team has forty-five minutes of team planning time, they should only assign topics for eight periods. This will leave the last period open. This requires that everyone give thought to how much time is essential for each topic.

It is fine for a team to finish a topic before the allotted time expires. The team simply moves on to the next topic. Do not put the time into other topics. Just finish early and have a bigger cushion of time to get back to class.

Teams should have a wind-up egg timer, and set the time for each topic. When the timer goes off, they know that they must move on to the next topic. BEWARE! It is not uncommon for teams to ignore the timer much like we ignore the morning alarm. Do not "hit the snooze button" and continue to discuss an item for additional time. The team has to move on, finished or not. The visual of the timer lets everyone know where they are and how much time is left, and helps them come to closure on time. Keeping pace will become more automatic, and even easily distracted team members will be more focused.

More Time Management Strategies

Teams that have two back-to-back planning periods should schedule their team meeting time as the last period of their two periods off. If they meet first, it is very likely that their meetings may spill over into their personal planning time. If teachers take their personal planning time first, that can never happen. Meeting as a team during the second part of a double planning time ensures team members will always have the advantage of their full individual planning time.

Of course, the problem then becomes getting everyone to team meetings on time. Everyone needs to understand the importance of being on time for team meetings. It is absolutely critical that all team members arrive on time and come prepared for the meeting. Phone-Call Phyllis will have to hang up, and Copy-Machine Chris will have to relinquish the copy machine so that they can get to the meetings on time.

The same strategy applies for team/parent conferences. When a parent calls for a conference, always put the conference at the end of the team meeting time. Then the conference cannot dominate the entire team time unless the team wants it to. For example: Suppose a team meeting time is from 9:00 AM to 9:45 AM, and a parent has called with a request to meet with the team. The team makes the decision that they need to meet for only twenty minutes with this parent. Simply tell the parent that the scheduled conference time is 9:20 AM. This will guarantee a team the first twenty minutes of meeting time before the conference. Teams may use that time to get ready for the conference, or to take care of some predetermined topics.

The most efficient and effective teams have predetermined topics for most days of the week. They always start their meetings with these topics. If a team wants to work on curriculum, they may decide to pre-dedicate the first three periods each Wednesday for curriculum. If they were to wait to do curriculum at the end of meetings, then there is always the chance that this area may be overlooked. If it comes first, then remaining time can be filled with the other issues.

If the parent mentioned earlier had called for a meeting on Wednesday, we know that we already have the first fifteen minutes dedicated to curriculum. So, we invite the parent to come after that, and tell him or her that we have thirty minutes in which to meet. Notice that we still try to leave the last five minutes open.

Time Management Questions

▲ What do we do when people outside the team, like an administrator, drop in during meetings and continually interrupt our team meeting time?

We mentioned an administrator because they are often the worst for interrupting a team. It is so convenient for administrators, counselors, etc. to visit. Teams need to let these people know that they are happy to meet with them, but they need to check the agenda to see if there is time for them. When they put themselves on the agenda, they need to know when their time will be. They do not have to sit through the entire meeting that way, but can be there when it is their time. If unexpected visits continue to be a problem, the team leader should meet with the person or persons to let them know how to be a part of a team meeting. School-wide training is beneficial as everyone will know the expectations of team meetings, and the procedures involved.

● What do we do if teachers are always showing up late?

One great thing to do is simply to make that a topic on the agenda. Without names, put the topic of team meeting time on an agenda to review how the time is being used. This should be a regular topic (in chapter eleven you will learn how to assess team success). If the problem persists, the team leader may meet with the tardy teachers individually. Ultimately, an administrator may have to be involved. The key is to not let it go on for very long. The sooner the team addresses the issue, the easier it is.

▲ What if one team member tends to dominate the discussion?

Establish a policy that each member present has the opportunity for a brief opening comment when a topic of discussion is started. Only after everyone has talked is the topic opened up for discussion.
Another useful idea developed by a team is to pass around a rubber ball. Only the person holding the ball can talk. They have to ask for the ball non-verbally, and there is a limited amount of time anyone can hold the ball. Also, the facilitator can help by keeping the conversation moving. If someone has not talked yet, the facilitator should ask the person for his or her thoughts. A good facilitator will keep the conversation moving without hurting anyone's feelings.

Practice Activity ■●▲

Take approximately fifteen minutes to brainstorm and list everything that you can think of that might come up in discussion during team meeting time. You may want to ask colleagues what items have come up during their team meeting time. Of course, if you are currently on a team, this would be best done as a team activity.

Determine which topics are appropriate for team meeting time. Some things like discipline have to be handled on an as-needed basis. Other topics, like curriculum and advisory can be scheduled for certain days of the week. List the items that could be pre-scheduled and designate each topic as weekly, monthly, quarterly, once a semester, and so on, depending on how often you feel it should be discussed. Also, decide which day or days would work best for each topic. For example: Advisory needs to be discussed every week. Fridays work well to discuss Advisory, to review the week, and to get the activities ready for the next week.

Finally, determine how many periods you would need to give to each topic. You will use this list to pick topics that will begin our agendas for each day. The team in the sample agenda (see Figure 2–1) had decided to discuss next week's schedule every Thursday for three periods. Any other agenda items for Thursdays will always follow the weekly discussion of the upcoming week's schedule. An example list (Figure 2–2) is provided to assist you with the activity.

WOW, What a Team!

EXAMPLE LIST

	Topic	Frequency	Day	Periods
1.	Student discipline	as needed		
2.	Team newsletter	quarterly	Thurs.	4
3.	Advisory	weekly	Fri.	2
4.	Positive parent calls	weekly	Mon.	1
5.	Tests	weekly	Mon.	1
6.	Curriculum	weekly	Wed.	2
7.	Field trips	as needed		
8.	Team calendar	weekly	Fri.	1
9.	Thumbs meetings	bi-weekly	Tues.	8
10.	Community service project	monthly	Thurs.	3
11.	Other topics . . .			

Figure 2–2. Sample example list.

Creating Agenda Sheets

Now it is time to put agenda sheets together for the team notebook. Some teams will do this a week at a time, while others will get the team notebook ready for a marking period at a time. Using your list of topics, create five agendas, one for each day of the week. A blank agenda is included for your use, (see Figure 2–4) after the Monday sample agenda that follows (Figure 2–3). Note that the Monday agenda shows that the team will discuss the positive phone calls for five minutes, and then create the weekly calendar for ten minutes. The team will fill in the rest of the periods as needed, understanding that the first fifteen minutes of each Monday are dedicated to the calls and the calendar. During the meeting, the scribe will keep the minutes on the agenda form.

While most days will have regularly scheduled topics, some days may not have predetermined topics and the entire agenda is left open to be filled by the team as needed. Each team will develop its own rhythm for setting their team meeting agenda.

SAMPLE TEAM MEETING AGENDA
AND MINUTES FOR MONDAYS
Date: /   /

Members present:

_____

_____

_____

Period	Item	Discussion/Action Taken
1.	Positive parent phone calls	Make a list
2.	Weekly calendar	
3.	" "	
4.		
5.		
6.		
7.		
8.		
9.		
10.		

Figure 2–3. Sample Monday agenda.

TEAM MEETING AGENDA
AND MINUTES
Date: /   /

Members present:

_____

_____

_____

Period	Item	Discussion/Action Taken
1.		
2.		
3.		
4.		
5.		
6.		
7.		
8.		
9.		
10.		

Figure 2–4. Blank agenda for activity.

CONCLUSION

John Wooden said, "Failure to prepare is preparing to fail". To get the most out of team meetings, teams must do some up-front preparation. The time a team puts in preparing for the meetings will come back to them many times over in time saved and productivity.

Chapter 3

Policies and Procedures

■●▲

"If you had but one wish, let it be for an idea."
—*Percy Sutton*

Chapter 3

Consistency is a crucial component to teaming. Establishing common policies and procedures is an essential element in meeting as a team. The ideal situation is to meet on a daily basis. Some schools give teams a class period of planning time to coordinate and plan. Other schools allow meetings two or three times a week. If a team does not have a time set aside at school, it is important to find time to meet. Some options are after school, before school, preparation time, lunchtime, or retreat days. It would be a worthwhile investment to convince the administration to allow for a retreat day for the team to meet off-site. This would enable team members to collaborate and make some major decisions. The retreat day must have a schedule and an agenda. Remember, this is productive work time—not a social meeting (see chapter two regarding agendas).

Retreat Day

Before the actual retreat day, the team leader should secure a meeting place and lunch. If necessary, fill out building use forms and see if administration will spring for the cost of lunch. If the school will not pay for lunch, decide if team members wish to go to lunch together, order in, or bring their own lunch. It would be nice to at least provide a morning snack and possibly afternoon refreshments.

An early retreat day provides an opportunity to coordinate team guidelines. If the retreat day is not an option, the team should discuss and develop consistent policies and procedures during the first team meetings. The sample agenda (Figure 3–1) is designated for a retreat day. The agenda could be broken down into sections if the plan is to cover the topics during team meeting time.

WOW, What a Team!

SAMPLE TEAM MEETING
RETREAT DAY

1. Policies and Procedures
   A. Late Work Policy
      1. One day late
      2. Two days late
      3. Credit vs. no credit
   B. Requirements
   C. Team Rules
      1. Hall
      2. Room

2. Team Newsletters
   A. Monthly
   B. Designate months to members

3. Advisory Activities
   A. Review topics to be covered
      1. Conflict
      2. Self-esteem
      3. Friendship
   B. Time schedule
      1. 15 minutes each day
      2. Problems
   C. Activities
      1. Share ideas
      2. Problems
      3. New resources

4. Technology
   A. Electronic grades
   B. Lab sign-up
   C. Integration into academic areas

5. Curriculum Partners
   A. Coordination of units for marking period
   B. State standards

6. Full-Group
   A. Summary of curriculums
   B. Other

Figure 3–1. Sample agenda for retreat day.

Develop a Plan

Whether policies are constructed during a regular team meeting, retreat day, or in-service day, it is critical to have a plan. The key areas to be discussed should be determined before the negotiation process begins. This will allow team members to do some research regarding the topics. Always remember that not everyone will enthusiastically embrace every idea, and that people should be able to openly express suggestions and opinions. This agreement will allow people to share ideas and opinions regarding policies.

Common Practices

Effective teams have consistent policies. There are seven topics that should be considered when addressing common practices among a team. These issues are:

▲ Team Meeting Time

● Homework Schedule

▲ Quiz and Test Schedule

● Grading Scale

▲ Late Policy

● Headings

▲ Discipline Policy

Team Meeting Time

Time is a critical component of effective team meetings. According to *Rottier (1996)*, common planning time for the team teachers is the core of an interdisciplinary structure. This time allows for consistency in planning of curriculum, conferences, and many other topics. *Forte and Schurr (1993)* state that interdisciplinary teaming is most effective when teachers on the same team have a common planning period. (See chapter two for getting the most out of your team meeting time.)

Team members need to know what the schedule is for team meetings. Teams that are fortunate enough to have a time during each school day to meet should have a specific time designated, and should begin promptly. If the team-planning hour begins at 1:55 PM, then that time—not 2:00 PM—is precisely when the meeting should begin. This also holds true for the teams that have a planning time two or three days a week. The teams that are not given time need to use creative ways to meet and plan. This meeting should begin on time and have a focus in order to accomplish what needs to be done. It is equally important to end meetings on time or there will be many frustrated individuals. Members should plan on being in attendance for the entire meeting. Effective teams need all members present for the full meeting to conduct business *(Rottier, 1996)*.

Points to Ponder

Please relate the questions below to your school day.

1. Do you have a set time to meet as a team?
2. If so, when is this time?
3. Do meetings begin on time?
4. Do they end on time?
5. If you do not have a daily planning time, list some alternative meeting times.

Homework Schedule

Coordinate homework and avoid overloading students with homework tasks on any given day (*Forte & Schurr, 1993*). A team homework schedule is a beneficial tool in the coordination process. This schedule will balance the homework load for students and is frequently complimented by parents. The first issue to address is the amount of homework that should be given at the team teachers' grade level. It is a good idea to find out what the other grade levels are expecting in the team's school. The homework policy should be in balance with the test policy. For example, if the homework night for math is Tuesday, then the quiz and test day for math should be on Wednesday.

A sample homework schedule is provided in Figure 3–2. A sixth grade team who decided that students should have no more than two subjects of homework a night originally developed this schedule. The philosophy of the team was that the students should have approximately an hour of academic homework per night. The general rule of thumb is approximately ten minutes of homework per grade level.

HOMEWORK SCHEDULE

Monday	Science	and	Social Studies
Tuesday	Math	and	Language Arts
Wednesday	Science	and	Reading
Thursday	Math	and	Social Studies
Friday	Reading	and	Language Arts

Figure 3–2. Sample homework schedule.

Practice Activity ■●▲

Use Figure 3–3 to relate the homework scheduling task to your team.

1. How much time should students spend on academic homework each night?

2. How many subjects should assign homework per night?

3. Fill in the following schedule regarding your appropriate team situation.

HOMEWORK SCHEDULE

Monday

Tuesday

Wednesday

Thursday

Friday

Figure 3–3. Sample homework schedule for activity.

Quiz and Test Schedule

Superior teams coordinate the administration of quizzes and tests (*Forte & Schurr, 1993*). A team quiz and test schedule is another beneficial tool in the coordination process. This schedule will balance the testing for students. The quiz and test schedule eliminates the problem of too many tests or quizzes on one day. The first issue to address is the amount of quizzes and tests that will be given on a particular day. The quiz and test policy should be coordinated with the homework policy.

The sixth grade team who developed the homework schedule (see Figure 3–2) developed the sample quiz and test schedule in Figure 3–4. As stated earlier, the philosophy of the team was that the students should have approximately an hour of academic homework per night. Their belief was that sixth grade students should not have more than two quizzes or tests per day. Please note that two quizzes or tests were not given each day, but if you were going to give a test you needed to plan according to the test schedule. If you absolutely needed a day assigned to another subject during the year, you would ask the teacher of that subject to trade test days for the week. Make it clear to students that the team may trade days for subjects to test if needed and that the team will provide advance notice.

WOW, What a Team!

The example team in this chapter followed the established homework and testing schedule for the entire school year. Some teams establish their homework and test schedules weekly. They set aside one or two periods (see chapter two) each Thursday or Friday to set the next week's homework and testing schedule. Each team will need to decide how frequently to set the schedules and then abide by them. Teams may select schedules according to the week, month, marking period, semester, or year. There are numerous possible combinations regarding schedules. You'll need to determine what is the best for the team teachers' students.

QUIZ AND TEST SCHEDULE

Monday	Reading	and	Language Arts
Tuesday	Science	and	Social Studies
Wednesday	Math	and	Language Arts
Thursday	Science	and	Reading
Friday	Math	and	Social Studies

Figure 3–4. Sample quiz and test schedule.

Practice Activity ■●▲

Use Figure 3–5 to relate the quiz and test scheduling task to your team.

1. What is the maximum number of quizzes or tests a student at your grade level should have in one day?

2. How many quizzes or tests do you give during a week?

3. How many quizzes or tests does your team give during a week?

4. Fill in the schedule (Figure 3–5) regarding your appropriate team situation.

QUIZ AND TEST SCHEDULE

Monday

Tuesday

Wednesday

Thursday

Friday

Figure 3–5. Sample quiz and test schedule for activity.

Grading Scale

Another commonality that works well on a team is the grading scale. Great teams establish common grading guidelines (*Forte & Schurr, 1993*). The concept of coordinated grading, like homework and testing, is beneficial for students and becomes an organizational tool. This strategy helps students by alleviating the need to keep track of many different grading scales. The grading scale issue is often an area of major discussion and negotiation on a team. A good start is to gather other grading scales. These may be from other schools or grade levels. Please note that many schools have a separate grading scale for math since some programs already have set scales. Other schools have school-wide scales that are predetermined by the principal or district. A sample grading scale is provided in Figure 3–6.

GRADING SCALE

A	93–100%
A-	90–92%
B+	87–89%
B	83–86%
B-	80–82%
C+	77–79%
C	73–76%
C-	70–72%
D+	67–69%
D	63–66%
D-	60–62%
E	0–59%

Figure 3–6. Sample grading scale.

Points to Ponder

1. Do you have a school-wide grading scale?

2. Do any subjects at your school have predetermined grading scales?

3. Do you have a common team grading scale?

4. If you do not have a team grading scale, consider approaching your team with the idea.

Late Policy

A common late policy will eliminate confusion on the part of students and parents. This policy will also reduce the comparison of why one teacher penalizes more than another does. This is a point where a team may have significantly different opinions.

The following situation demonstrates one way to effectively deal with the individual opinions of team members. There were eight teachers on a particular team. All but one member on the team wanted the late policy for homework to be 10% off the first day late and 0% (no credit) on the assignment after the first day. The lone teacher wanted to give the students 10% off the first day late, 50% off the second day late, and 0% (no credit) on the assignment after the second day. The one teacher stood strong the issue and the team did as well. The final agreement was that they would print in the team handbook under homework, "10% off if one day late". The students would be told in classes about the policy and the lone teacher would do the second day at 50%, where the rest would give a 0% on the second day.

Points to Ponder

1. Do you think this was a good agreement for the team?

2. Does the agreement demonstrate consistency and team unity?

3. Must everyone agree all the time?

4. Does your team have a late policy?

5. What do you use for a late policy?

Headings

Students of teaming teachers should know the team's expectation for headings. Teams should support a standard paper heading (*Forte & Schurr, 1993*). This point may seem minimal, but it will save time and confusion for the students. It should be clear where to write their name or any other required information for all classes. Once the team has determined the proper heading, it would be helpful to display the expectation on poster board for the students. A sample heading is provided in Figure 3–7. All requirements are in the upper right hand corner of the paper.

Name
Date
Subject
Hour

Figure 3–7. Sample heading.

The team should be able to express ideas and agree on a heading for students. It is a good idea to look at other grade levels in the team school at this point and see if headings could be coordinated school-wide.

Points to Ponder

1. What is your required heading?

2. Does your team have the same heading requirement?

3. Are you aware of what other grade levels in your building require?

Discipline Procedure

Discipline is a significant issue faced by educators that relates directly to the safety of students. It is a necessity that the school has an established discipline policy. This policy may be sufficient for a team. Nevertheless, if the team is going to establish a distinct discipline policy, it should be printed in a handbook for students. According to *Forte and Schurr (1993)*, competent interdisciplinary teams construct a handbook for students and parents. The handbook needs to include the common policies and procedures.

The team should use the school discipline policy as a guide to their approach. Teams need to discuss discipline issues and consequences for each action. Put downs, disruptive behavior, drugs, physical assault, and stealing are issues that teachers cannot ignore.

A sample team discipline policy is shown below.

Team Seven Discipline Policy

Students will be expected to follow the school rules as outlined in the school handbook along with the following team policy.

▲ Respect others and their property

● Bring materials to class

▲ Put downs are not tolerated*

● No gum chewing in class

▲ No hats in class

One team has a fun addition to this rule. If a student is put down, he or she is entitled to three put ups. The student who put down someone must state three positive things (put ups) about the student they put down.

Practice Activity

Relate the following questions and task to your situation.

1. What is the school discipline policy?

2. Where is the school policy printed?

3. Does your team have a discipline policy?

4. What is your classroom discipline policy?

5. Brainstorm and list possible team rules below.

▲

●

▲

●

▲

●

▲

●

▲

●

▲

●

CONCLUSION

Once the policies and procedures have been determined, it is crucial to share them with students and parents. A team handbook is an effective method of communication. The handbook should include the names of team members, team policies, team schedule of classes, conference options, and special dates and events.

There are a variety of problems that can result from not creating consistency on a team. Teams eliminate a lot of confusion for students and parents when procedures are aligned. If team members have separate grading scales, headings, policies, etc. the students need to learn numerous pieces of information instead of one set. Also, having different grading scales opens the door for parents and students to play teachers against one another.

The quiz and test schedule is important to coordinate for the sake of learning, this way the students can prepare for a small number of tests and quizzes on any given day instead of all of the testing on one day. The commonalties demonstrate unity and showcase the team as one, as well as to help reduce parental comparison of team members.

The collective practices among a team strengthen the effectiveness of the team. The similarities create a cohesive team. It is easy for students, parents, staff, and the administration to see team harmony in situations where there is coordination and planning.

Chapter 4

Student Recognition

―――――――――――――――――― ■●▲

*"Motivation is when your dreams
put on work clothes."*
—Ben Franklin

Chapter 4

Highlighting student achievement at the middle level is important. There are numerous benefits to recognition programs. Some of the positive outcomes associated with recognition often include improved student behavior, increased self-esteem, supportive school environments, and parental support. According to *Fisher (1991),* students who have been praised are often better behaved, more motivated, and more productive than their peers who have been discouraged. There are a variety of techniques to recognize students. Classroom, team, or school-wide programs are recognition methods that prove to be beneficial. Listed below are ideas to promote the positive.

Classroom Recognition Ideas ■●▲

The classroom teacher can easily implement these recognition ideas. They are low cost for the teacher and effective for the students.

Awards

The awards may be issued in the form of a certificate. The certificates may be used for a variety of reasons. Some teachers award a "Best Test" certificate to the student who scores the highest on the test. Other teachers reward students for earning a 90% or higher on the test. The awards could be for projects, homework, tests, quizzes, behavior, or any creative idea. A sample certificate is shown in Figure 4–1.

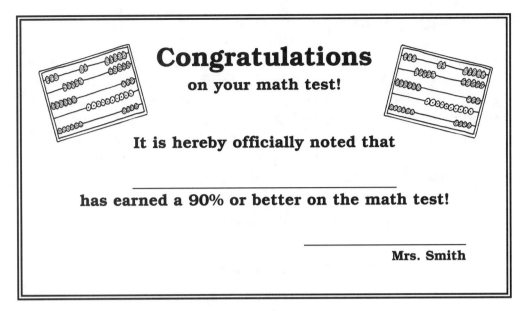

Congratulations

on your math test!

It is hereby officially noted that

_____

has earned a 90% or better on the math test!

_____

Mrs. Smith

Figure 4–1. Sample math certificate.

Working Bulletin Boards

A great idea is to have bulletin boards that are learning centers. These boards are enrichment activities that challenge the students. A "Problem of the Week" board is an activity that works well at the middle school level. A problem is posted each week and students are given four days to guess the answer. The answer is posted on the fifth day. Students who arrive at the correct solution have their names placed on the bulletin board and receive extra credit.

Sample Problem (Answer provided on page 67.)

> *Where should the number 10 be placed to complete the sequence?*
>
> **8, 5, 4, 9, 1, 7, 6, 2**

The Birthday Board

The birthday board will eventually acknowledge every student in the classroom. Decorate an area or bulletin board in the room. Each month list the names and dates of each student having a birthday. The original decorations may remain on the board all year, just replace the paper with the names of students each month. Summer birthdays (June, July, and August) should be posted during the month of June.

Sample sheet with birthdays listed below.

☆May Birthdays!!!☆

Suzy Smith	3rd
John Doe	7th
Jack Johnson	14th
Becky Adams	22nd
Sara Russell	25th

Team Recognition Ideas ——————————————— ■●▲

The teachers on the team will need to determine which recognition strategies they wish to utilize. Teams are able to highlight student achievement and demonstrate team unity once a decision is made on which recognition techniques to use.

Growing Tree

A good place for the team "growing tree" is in the team hall. The tree is constructed of paper, and leaves are added as students are recognized for various reasons. Each leaf has the name of a student printed on it. Examples of recognition may vary from improvement in behavior to an overall positive attitude in class. Teachers should fill out a form (Figure 4–2) when they recognize a student, and place the form in the designated area in the team room. A specified team member is responsible for hanging the leaves each week. The forms are sent home in report cards at the end of each marking period. The leaves are taken down after each marking period, and a new tree begins.

Growing Tree

Student Recognized _____

Reason for Recognition

_____

_____

_____

Teacher _____ Date _____

©2001 by Incentive Publications, Inc. Nashville, TN.

Figure 4–2. Sample Growing Tree form.

Thumbs Up Award

These awards recognize students for their behavioral and academic effort (see chapter five).

Team Smile

Each teacher should have access to smile cards (Figure 4–3). Smiles are given out to students who are putting forth the extra effort. Smiles may be handed out for improvement in behavior, grades, or just doing a good job in the classroom. A drawing is held on Friday where five of the selected students are rewarded with a treat, such as a candy bar.

```
Smile—You're Great!
Thanks for doing a super job!

Student Name  _____

Teacher  _____

                         Date _____

©2001 by Incentive Publications, Inc. Nashville, TN.
```

Figure 4–3. Smile card.

School Recognition Ideas ━━━━━━━━━━━━ ■●▲

Programs are often implemented by administration. However, individual teachers or teaching teams are generally able to recommend new approaches and evaluate existing programs.

Student of the Month

Staff members nominate students each month. A sample nomination form is provided in Figure 4–4. There are different methods to approach this concept. Some teams encourage each teacher to nominate a student, while others select one boy and one girl each month per team. Each team must determine the best procedure for nominating students. The student selection process is based on criteria established by the school. It is important that the criteria be meaningful and that a wide variety of students are represented. A sample for criteria is listed below.

Sample Criteria for Student of the Month
A. Considerate to others
B. Maintains high standards of citizenship
C. Works well in class
D. Demonstrates a positive attitude
E. Demonstrates respect
F. Is responsible

Student of the Month

Student Nominated _____

Teacher_____ Date _____

Reason for nomination

_____

©2001 by Incentive Publications, Inc. Nashville, TN.

Figure 4–4. Sample form.

Excellence Cards

Excellence cards (Figure 4–5) are part of a school-wide recognition program. Staff members may issue these to students when they catch students doing the right thing. Students making the extra effort or doing extraordinary things would earn excellence cards. The students save the cards until they acquire a certain number and then they see the principal for the reward. Ideas for prizes could be a water bottle for six cards, a t-shirt for twelve cards, and a sweatshirt for eighteen cards. Cards may be school-specific such as Viking Shields (in the shape of a shield), Eagle Wings (in the shape of a wing), Panther Paws (in the shape of a paw), etc.

Excellence Card

Student Name _____

Teacher _____

Date _____

©2001 by Incentive Publications, Inc. Nashville, TN.

Figure 4–5. Sample excellence card.

Practice Activity ■●▲

Please answer the following questions.

1. Do you award students in your classroom?

2. If so, how?

3. Does your team have a recognition program?

4. If so, what is the program?

5. Does your school have a recognition program?

6. If so, what is the program?

7. You will be developing a certificate to use in your classroom. Will the award be for a quiz, test, assignment, or something else?

Use Figure 4-6 to draw a rough sketch of how you would like the certificate to look.

Figure 4–6. Blank form for activity certificate.

CONCLUSION

It is important to recognize students in meaningful ways, especially at the middle school level. Educators strive to motivate their students, build self-esteem, and help develop cooperative contributors though the use of recognition programs. Once a team decides what strategies work best for their team, they should put a personal spin on them. There are a variety of computer programs to generate certificates, banners, cards, etc. to help with the creative process.

Students are often eager to participate and work hard if they are motivated. There are various forms of motivation. This lesson has highlighted some of the recognition techniques, but remember to instill an internal love of learning with your enthusiasm! Try to laugh and enjoy your time with the students.

Dorothy frequently uses different types of recognition in her classroom. This chapter concludes with one of her experiences.

Turtle-Grams

I noticed a seventh grade teacher in my building awarding certificates to students who did well on assignments, quizzes, projects, or tests. In fact, sometimes this teacher would hand out his award for other reasons such as doing good things or whatever he deemed appropriate. The reason I was so aware of what was going on in another team was through the students. The students were in my class the previous year. They would run to my room to show me the "Turtle-Grams". (The teacher's last name rhymed with turtle and he collected turtles.)

I was amazed at how excited the students were over a small piece of paper. They gave me a running tally of how many they and other classmates acquired. The certificate just read "Turtle-Gram— given to (student name) for (reason)." The award was handwritten. Keep in mind he is a math teacher—not an art teacher.

The students absolutely loved the award. I later realized it was not just the piece of paper that the student enjoyed. They relished the recognition. Mr. Turtle made a big deal out of good academics and behavior. I can only imagine how the parents of those children felt when they came rushing home with the Turtle-Gram.

I later decided to begin my own reward system in class. It is important to recognize all areas, not just academic. One of the rewards I chose was to administer certificates for 90% or higher on tests, and I would give a million dollar pencil to any student who earned 100%. This was a highlight for the students and my timing was perfect, as "Who Wants to be a Millionaire" was a popular show that year. Note—Always remember to have enough of whatever you choose to give to students. I ran out of million-dollar pencils in May and tried to hand out hippo pencils that said "Jogging to the Beat." This was not a good idea. What was I thinking? Needless to say, I have ordered a three-year supply of money pencils.

*The answer to the sample problem on page 59: Between the six and the two. (The numbers are in alphabetical order.)

Chapter 5

Coordinating with Administrators and Counselors

■●▲

"The art of being wise is the art of knowing what to overlook."
—William James

Chapter 5

Think for a moment about how many students each individual teacher will see in any given day. A four-person team with an average class size of 27 sees a total of 108 students. It is very difficult to discuss each of the 108 students on an individual basis regularly. As was mentioned earlier, teams often complain that they spend 90% of their time discussing 10% of their students. There is a process, however, that will allow a team to discuss the success of every student on the team by name and to recognize his or her efforts.

When teams work together with administrators and counselors, miracles can happen. The Thumbs Up meetings discussed in this chapter will demonstrate a way for teams to coordinate their efforts with administrators and counselors to meet the needs of every student on the team. Another bonus is that these meetings are quick and easy. Most teams conduct a Thumbs Up meeting every two weeks.

The purpose of this chapter is to help teams do two things for their students. First, teams will learn how to identify and recognize student progress. Teams will also learn how to identify student needs and provide interventions in a timely manner. The Thumbs Up meetings give teams a way to do both.

Thumbs Up Meetings

The Thumbs Up activity is a way for teams to discuss the progress of each of their students by name in five areas of criteria. With the support of the administrators and counselors, the team will designate follow-up interventions as needed for students. It is an absolute non-negotiable requirement that an administrator and the counselor assigned to the team attend the Thumbs Up meetings. There are three main components to develop an understanding of a Thumbs Up meeting. First are the five criteria that are considered to review each student. Then, there is the process of how to run the Thumbs Up meeting. And finally, the recognition and follow-up interventions that are built into the process.

The Criteria

There are five criteria that everyone at the Thumbs Up meeting must consider in regard to each student. At the beginning of the meetings (described in the next section), each teacher will indicate with a Thumbs Up if students are meeting the criteria listed below. On the other hand, each teacher will indicate with a Thumbs Down if students are not meeting the criteria.

1. Academic — Is the student performing at or above his or her expected level of performance? The key words here are <u>expected level of performance</u>. This criterion is not the level of achievement so much as doing the work that is expected. For example, a "D" student would meet the criteria for success if he or she were doing "D" work. Handing in all of the work and doing the best that he or she can do is the measure of success here.

2. Student Behavior — Is the student following the team's discipline plan, or is the student causing problems with inappropriate behavior? Appropriate behavior meets the criteria; any other behavior does not. Any student with a discipline referral since the last Thumbs Up meeting could not meet the criteria. Students just beginning to cause problems with classroom disruptions, etc. and are just at that pre-referral stage are also not meeting this criteria.

3. Social — Is the student fitting in with his or her peer group? If the student is fitting in with his or her peer group as appropriately as can be expected, then he or she would meet the criteria. If they are being picked on or ostracized in a way that causes concern, then the student does not meet the criteria for successful peer interaction. Sometimes students will remove themselves from their social peers. If it were at a point of concern, this would also call for a Thumbs Down.

4. Emotional — Does the student appear to be okay emotionally (at least as okay as a middle level student can be), or is the student struggling emotionally? Perhaps a teacher has seen the student crying, and he or she will not share what is wrong. If the student seems to be okay emotionally, then he or she meets the criteria. If a teacher has concerns about the student's emotional stability, then he or she does not meet the criteria for emotional success.

5. Personal — Is the student or anyone else doing anything that could be hurtful or harmful to the student? If a teacher has any concerns about physical or emotional abuse, the use of drugs, alcohol, or self-mutilation, then the student would not meet the criteria for personal success. If there do not appear to be things that are causing personal harm to the student, teachers would indicate a Thumbs Up.

Part One

Thumbs Up meetings are run in two parts. In part one, the team leader reads out the names of the students on the team. Usually the names are grouped and read by their advisory or homeroom assignment. Each teacher considers the success of each student in all five of the criteria areas.

If a teacher has a concern in any one or more of the areas, that teacher indicates that by showing a Thumbs Down. If the teacher has no concerns about the student in any of the areas, he or she will indicate that with a Thumbs Up. The meeting will proceed until every student on the team has been called out.

The administrator will have a stack of the Thumbs Up certificates to fill out (see Figure 5–2). If a student does not have any Thumbs Down (some teams will allow one Thumb Down), then the administrator writes the student's name on one of the certificates. As soon as the administrator begins to write the name, another name is called. There is no hesitation between names, and no one is allowed to speak except for the person reading the names.

The counselor will be recording any Thumbs Down that teachers indicate for any of the students. The counselor usually has a duplicate list of the names and follows along as the names are read. If a student receives a Thumbs Down, the counselor makes a note of who gave the Thumb Down on his or her sheet. The meeting will progress as fast as the administrator and counselor can write.

During part one, it is very important to note that no one is allowed to talk except the person, usually the team leader, who is reading the names of the students. Teachers may not try to explain their Thumbs Up or Down at this time, and as said before, there should be no discussion at all. It is often reported that not talking is the most difficult part of the process.

At the end of part one, there will be a stack of filled out certificates completed by the administrator and the counselor's list of those students receiving the Thumbs Down. The counselor will facilitate part two of the meeting by going back over the lists and reading the names of students that had received one or more Thumbs Down.

Part Two

The counselor facilitates part two. He or she begins to read back the names of the students that had received a Thumbs Down from the teachers. The names will be put on the intervention form (see Figure 5–3). During part two, teachers are expected to say why they indicated a Thumbs Down for their students. They must indicate which of the criteria areas they are concerned about for each student to whom they gave a Thumbs Down.

As each name is read, the teachers will indicate their concerns, and the person responsible for the intervention area will be determined. The area of concern will determine the person responsible for the intervention (Figure 5–1). The person that will be responsible for the intervention phase will take notes about that student.

WOW, What a Team!

If the area of concern is academic, the student's advisor will be responsible. The notes may include such things as incomplete work, late work, or poor preparation. The administrator will be responsible for behavioral concerns. The administrator will make notes of what behaviors are going on in which classes. The counselor will be responsible for social, emotional, or personal concerns. The counselor will note the behaviors a teacher has seen or heard to cause these concerns.

CONCERN	PERSON RESPONSIBLE
1. Academic	1. Advisor
2. Behavior	2. Administrator
3. Social	3. Counselor
4. Emotional	4. Counselor
5. Personal	5. Counselor

Figure 5–1. Sample of persons responsible for follow-up interventions depending on the area of concern.

If a student did not get a Thumbs Up certificate because of social, emotional, or personal concerns, then a Thumbs Up certificate if filled out at this point. Certificates are only withheld for academic and disciplinary problems. As we do not discuss particular students during part one, we indicate a Thumbs Down to initiate the discussion that happens in part two.

Sometimes teachers will indicate a Thumbs Down in part one for academic or behavioral problems—but withholding the certificate is not intended. The teachers may say that they want the student to receive the award, but they still want the administrator to talk with the student and let them know if the behavior persists, they will not receive the award next time.

The Follow-Up Interventions

Each of the persons that took the notes for each of the areas noted will be responsible for the follow-up interventions.

The student's advisor will meet with the student the next morning during Advisory, or one of the classes, to discuss the student's academic issues. The advisor and team may decide to do an academic contract with the student, or it may be just a matter of informing the student of make-up work or missing work.

Most teams have the student take something home to the parents for their signature indicating the missing work, or other academic concerns that were the cause for the Thumbs Down. Many teams also have the advisor call home to inform the parents. However it is accomplished, parents should be notified about academic issues.

The administrator will talk to each student with behavioral issues. This is usually done in the hallways or at lunch. The administrator finds the student, and talks to him or her about their behavior. The administrator can be very specific about the behaviors to be corrected and his or her expectations for improvement. For most students this type of intervention can avoid later write-ups that take much more time. This is a proactive approach to discipline.

The administrator may facilitate the development of a behavior contract between the student and his or her teaming teachers. Since this may be in the early stages of the discipline process, the team and the administrator will decide if bringing in the parents is needed. Most teams inform the parents either by note or call from a team member or the administrator.

The counselor will be responsible to follow-up on any social, emotional, or personal concerns the teachers have. The counselor will look into the student's situation, and take appropriate action. The counselor will inform the team about what was going on with the student. Counselors get more appropriate and timely referrals in this process than team members.

The counselor will contact the parents as is appropriate in each case. Since the Thumbs Up certificates are never withheld for difficulties in this area, students do not know that they have been referred to the counselor.

Go through your class lists and evaluate each of your students relative to the criteria used in a Thumbs Up meeting. (See pages 71–72 for the criteria.) If you are a member of a team, you might request that your teammates run an actual Thumbs Up meeting with your administrator and counselor. Use the Follow-up Interventions form (Figure 5–3) to record the Thumbs Down students, the person responsible, and the intervention taken.

THUMBS UP

is awarded to _____

_____   _____   _____

_____   _____   _____

_____   _____   _____

©2001 by Incentive Publications, Inc. Nashville, TN.

Figure 5-2. The Thumbs Up Award.

FOLLOW-UP INTERVENTIONS

Student Name	Person Responsible for Intervention Taken	Intervention
1.		
2.		
3.		
4.		
5.		
6.		
7.		
8.		
9.		
10.		

Figure 5–3. The follow-up interventions sheet.

CONCLUSION

Thumbs Up meetings demonstrate the highest level of collaboration between teams, administrators, and counselors. All students are mentioned by name, and have the opportunity to have their efforts recognized. In addition to student recognition, the process also calls for any needed interventions, which are put in place for students in a timely manner.

Schools are often reactive in dealing with students. The Thumbs Up process is a proactive approach for schools working to meet the social, emotional, and academic needs of early adolescents. It is highly unlikely for any student to get lost in the shuffle with this process in place.

The Thumbs Up Award is both motivational and informational. The award is motivational for some, and informational for all. While receiving this award will motivate some students, all students will receive valuable and timely feedback about their progress.

WOW, What a Team!

Chapter 6

Team Conferences with Students and Parents

■●▲

"It's hard to beat a person who never gives up."
—*Babe Ruth*

Chapter 6

Teams often use meeting time to discuss students' academic, behavioral, and social needs. During these discussions, teachers generally discover similar characteristics of concern among specific students. Team members are able to address issues and determine intervention strategies. It is common practice at the middle level to hold student, parent, and team conferences. Parents or teachers may request conferences. The key to an effective conference is to be prepared and proactive.

All team members should be present during the scheduled conference. It is irrelevant if one teacher is not as concerned about the situation as others are. They still need to be there in support of the team. More often than not, team members see the same behaviors consistently. The decision whether to have the student involved with a parent conference is at the discretion of the team. Some parents will request that their child be present while others may not realize that their child could be involved. Regardless, it is a good idea to have the student, parent, and team discuss the issue and agree on a plan of action.

WOW, What a Team!

Getting the Conference Started

Prior to the conference, a contact must be made with the parents or by the parents. A date and time should be set that is convenient for all involved. It is essential to begin the conference on a positive note. Beginning the meeting with the student's strengths helps in establishing a good working relationship between the team, and the parents. During the conference, the team must be straightforward and share their reasons for concern. This information should be observable in work samples, scores, and records. Always remember to discuss the concerns as well as the strengths of the student.

The conference needs to be organized and have a purpose. One member of the team should be designated as the facilitator for the conference. The facilitator will provide direction. A team conference form is a tool that will help the team stay on task. This form will document concerns and help formulate a course of action. A sample form is provided in Figure 6–1.

TEAM CONFERENCE FORM

Student's Name _____ Date _____

Reason for Conference _____

_____

_____

Parent Concerns _____

_____

_____

_____

Team Concerns _____

_____

_____

_____

Student Concerns _____

_____

_____

_____

Action Plan

▲ _____

● _____

▲ _____

● _____

Follow-up Discussion

When? _____ Student _____

Who will contact parents? _____

Signatures

Parent _____   _____

Team Member _____   _____

Team Member _____   _____

Administrator _____ Counselor _____

Copies to: _____   _____

Figure 6–1. Sample team conference form.

Accessible Documentation

The Team Conference Form should be retained in a file or three-ring notebook for documentation. The team leader may be the individual responsible for the record keeping of conferences. It is extremely important that this information is filed and easily accessible. If another conference is scheduled, a team should use the first form as a guide. Teams must follow through with the action plan or the process will not reach full potential.

Keys to an Effective Student/Parent Conference:

A. Schedule the meeting in advance so the time is suitable for both parents and the team.

The idea is to set a positive tone from the beginning, so demonstrate flexibility by accommodating the parents' schedule. Parents will be very appreciative if the team is cooperative and shows understanding.

B. Document concerns via observation, records, scores, and work samples.

The team should have materials available at the conference to show the parents. Bring papers, tests, records, reports, or anything else that could help the parents understand the team's point of view. It is crucial to have documentation on the area of concern. If a team has implemented "Thumbs Up" meetings (see chapter five), the information from these meetings will be helpful during a team conference with parents and students. The team is setting themselves up for failure if they base the conference on personal opinion.

C. Discuss the student's strengths in addition to the concerns.

No one wants to hear only negatives regarding their behavior or work. Inform the student and parents of the good things the student has achieved and the capabilities of the student. The goal is to improve or encourage student effort through positive reinforcement.

D. Stay focused on the issues for the conference.

It is easy to become sidetracked in any situation especially when there is a group of people at a meeting. In order to run an effective conference there must be direction. A good tool to use is a team conference form. A sample is provided. (See Figure 6–1.)

E. Develop a plan of action.

The team, parents, and student should make an agreement on what the next course of action will be. This plan will hopefully improve the current situation. The steps for this procedure should be written on the team conference form.

F. Follow the action plan consistently.

Once all members agree on the action plan, all team members and parents must follow through with the agreement. The student will soon realize that everyone is working together. By being consistent and following the course of action, the student understands that they must be accountable for their end of the agreement.

G. Set a contact date for follow-up discussion.

The team initiates the next step, which is a follow-up conversation. A date should be determined at the conference when the parents will be contacted again. The team leader or homeroom teacher will be the contact person. This process can be a phone contact or another conference, depending on the needs of the student.

Practice Assignment ■●▲

Use the box below (Figure 6–2) to construct a form that will work for your team. Consider whether you will have team members as the only staff present, or if you are going to include counselors and administrators.

Figure 6–2. Practice form.

CONCLUSION

Conferences are an integral part of the home/school communication process. There are a variety of methods to conduct conferences. Teachers and teams must decide the most appropriate technique to achieve the best results. As we have worked with teams across the country we have accumulated the most frequently asked questions.

1. *Are conferences necessary?*

   Yes. Avoiding parents does not make the situation any easier. The quicker you establish a good parent-teacher relationship, the better your odds of a supportive relationship from home.

2. *Where should the conference take place?*

   Some schools have required meeting areas such as the gymnasium, team room, or cafeteria. It would be beneficial if you could meet with parents in the classroom. This would allow parents to see what the room is like and give you the opportunity to show student activities that highlight the classroom.

   Arrange chairs in a circle or sit at a table where everyone can be seen and heard easily. Avoid one teacher at his or her desk with everyone else in desks or chairs. No one should give the impression of being dominant or not as interested by where they position themselves.

3. *How should I begin the conference?*

Always begin on a positive note! Offer the parents something to drink and have snacks available. Highlight the strengths of the student. This will let the parents know you are concerned and recognize the talents of their child. Once you have established a comfortable environment, proceed with the details of the conference.

4. *Does the entire team really need to be present at the conference?*

It is important to have all team members present if possible. This will enable parents and team members to see if the concerns are similar for all classes. Meeting as a team also demonstrates coordination and offers support for members.

5. *What if I know the conference will be a rough one?*

Remember to start out on a positive note. Offer parents refreshments at the beginning to ease the tension of the situation. Let parents know you care about this student, and begin with the strengths of their child. If this is a team conference, you will have other members there to support you. However, if you are meeting alone and are uncomfortable, ask an administrator to be there.

6. *When should students be present?*

This question depends on how a school structures conferences. If doing student-led conferences, each student would accompany their parent. Some schools involve the students if there is an area of concern (examples—missing homework, behavioral concern, low tests, etc.). It is a good idea to meet with the parents before bringing in the student to establish some home and school expectations.

WOW, What a Team!

7. *What should I take with me?*

Be prepared! Teachers should have notes on each child. Student grades and missing work should be discussed. Observations made in class regarding social aspects pertaining to the child need to be addressed as well. Parents enjoy seeing their child's work and pictures. Teachers could have samples of student work, and that would be helpful in establishing their position or demonstrating what the student is capable of achieving. Taking photos of the activities throughout the year and having an album for viewing is a special treat for parents who are unable to attend many of the school events.

8. *What if one parent blames the other parent?*

It is important not to criticize a parent. There are a variety of circumstances that exist with married couples and single parents. Try to meet with both parents in hopes of better understanding the student's home environment. Focus on the student and what would benefit him or her.

9. *How do I end the conference?*

The facilitator should summarize the points discussed at the conference. Share with the parents what the team's plan is for the child's progress and growth. Also, alert parents to upcoming activities and events in which their child will be involved. Ask parents if they have any additional questions or concerns. Lastly, make sure to thank them for attending the conference!

Chapter 7

Informative Newsletters

■●▲

*"There's as much risk in doing nothing
as doing something."*
—Trammel Crow

Chapter 7

A communication tool utilized by many teams is a newsletter. The team leader needs to take on the responsibility of writing newsletters or delegating this task to a willing team member. Constructing the newsletter requires time and energy. If the team does not feel it is appropriate to have one person accountable for this task, members may rotate the responsibility for each newsletter. The team must determine how often newsletters will be sent home. Some schools send home team newsletters each marking period with report cards, while others do monthly newsletters with a theme for the month.

Newsletters should show highlights since the last newsletter and contain any upcoming events for students and parents. Each subject may have designated space on the newsletter to alert parents to upcoming events. This is a good opportunity to promote team interdisciplinary units and student accomplishments. Special schedules, assemblies, field trips, or days off are also important to include in the newsletter.

Constructing the Newsletter

The newsletter should be a prescheduled weekly topic for team meetings (see chapter two) with two periods dedicated to the newsletter. The person responsible for the newsletter gets weekly updates, ideas, and information from his or her teammates. This will make the task easier for the person putting the newsletter together, and ensure that everyone in the team has input.

WOW, What a Team!

A word processor may be used for the newsletter. It will enhance the newsletter if graphics are utilized. There are programs you may purchase to assist your team in developing newsletters. These programs are easy to use and produce a professional product. Most often one page, front and back, is plenty for a monthly newsletter. A sample newsletter is shown in Figure 7–1.

Always remember that the newsletter is a public relations tool and a representation of the team. In order to be taken seriously, the team needs to produce a quality product. Make sure the document is free from spelling and grammatical errors. The person constructing the newsletters should try to use a word processing program that checks for spelling and grammar and have a colleague preview the work. Try to avoid educational jargon in the newsletter, as it is often confusing and intimidating for parents.

Keep in mind that information printed in the newsletter must be accurate. If a team is planning a communication interdisciplinary unit and then prints the information, they must actually follow through with that unit. Use a positive writing style and overall approach to the newsletter. Highlight the great things taking place within the team and in the entire school. Remember, the newsletter is a chance to share the news and showcase accomplishments. Use this tool to the team's advantage.

SIXTH GRADE TEAM
October Newsletter

Thank You

We are very appreciative of the students' hard work and parental support during the first marking period. We are seeing steady growth in academic and study skills and want to encourage the students to continue using their homework organizers, the academic assistance time after school, and the homework hotline.

We also want to thank the parents and community for their support of the Bond Issue to renovate the Middle School, which will provide improved educational opportunities for our students.

Math Fair

The Sixth Grade Team is in the process of coordinating a Math Fair. Students will work in specialty groups to expand their interest in a specific math area. The Math Fair is scheduled for November 17. Sixth grade students will present projects to the fifth grade students during this event.

A big thank you to the Foundation for the mini-grant in support of the Math Fair! On November 14, the sixth grade students will be participating in a presentation by Mr. John Doe. His program, "Rising Stars", emphasizes teamwork and sharing.

Science Update

Students can look forward to dissecting a cow's heart, in conjunction with their study of the circulatory system. There will also be a special assembly on December 12, on the topic of Science and Sports.

Figure 7–1. Sample newsletter.

WOW, What a Team!

Reading Corner

Students are preparing for an autobiography or biography book report. The timeline for this report is as follows:

October 3rd—autobiography or biography book must be chosen
October 24th—students should be finished reading their book
November 7th—rough draft (index cards/outline of report) due
November 14th—oral reports will be given during this week

Directions, requirements, and suggestions for this book report will be discussed in class on October 10th.

United Way

During the week of October 10th, students will participate in a community service project for United Way. Homerooms will collect loose change from students, and the homeroom that collects the most money will receive a pizza party from the Student Council.

Ice Skating Parties

Skating parties held at The Ice Center cost $3.00 at the door.
October 13   4:00 - 6:00 p.m.
March 10   4:00 - 6:00 p.m.
May 12   4:00 - 6:00 p.m.

Dances

Dances held at Middle School Gym cost $3.00 at the door.
April 14   6:00 - 8:00 p.m.
May 19   6:00 - 8:00 p.m.

Thought for the School Year
Positive Preparation Promotes Peak Performance.

Figure 7–1, continued. Sample newsletter.

Using the Internet for Assistance

What did we do before the Internet? How did we manage without computers? Many practical ideas are now at teachers' fingertips. There are a variety of online resources to assist in developing a newsletter. There are numerous sites available ranging from professional newsletters developed by companies specializing in this area, to educators who constructed their own newsletters. If the team's school has a website, consider posting the team newsletter on it. This would allow the information to be easily accessible to parents who use the computer.

The following site is beneficial when creating a team newsletter.

http://schoolnewsletters.com/

Please visit the following sites for additional sample school newsletters.

▲ http://www.wayland.k12.ma.us/middle_school/newsletters/newsletters_index.htm

● http://avalon.epsb.net/

▲ http://www.education-world.com/

Practice Activity ■●▲

You will be constructing a team newsletter for this activity. What will be the name of your newsletter?

(Examples—Team Eight, Viking News, Caught in the Middle) Determine what the major areas will be for your team to have on the newsletter. Using the template, construct a newsletter of upcoming events at your grade level to share with your team.

Name of Newsletter_____

Date _____

Topic _____
Information relating to topic:

Topic _____
Information relating to topic:

Topic _____
Information relating to topic:

Topic _____
Information relating to topic:

CONCLUSION

Newsletters are an effective method of communication. Team newsletters are another occasion to demonstrate team unity. The information in the newsletters should convey a positive message to readers. Many parents are unable to attend school events that occur during the school day and a newsletter provides parents with the current happenings of the school. Determine the frequency of team newsletters and concentrate on positive and accurate information.

Chapter 8

Flexible Scheduling

■●▲

"This thing we call 'failure' is not the falling down, but the staying down."
—Mary Pickford

Chapter 8

There are many sacred cows in education. One of the most sacred is the bell schedule. The truth is that there is no perfect time frame for all lessons. We know that teachers should use a variety of instructional strategies if they are to meet the needs of all their students. Different instructional strategies require different time frames. However, in most schools (even middle schools), all classes tend to begin and end at the same time. The usual class period is too short for most active involvement instructional strategies. One of the biggest roadblocks to creative instruction is the bell schedule. What we will try to do in this chapter is demonstrate how to flex your schedule to accommodate instruction and assessment.

Another sacred cow is student grouping. Once a student is assigned to a social studies class with twenty-seven other students, the twenty-eight of them will be in the same social studies class for the entire year. Teachers use different cooperative learning groups in each class. There is no reason that students could not be regrouped between classes, and many reasons that regrouping between classes should happen. We will demonstrate when it is appropriate to regroup classes, and how to make it happen.

The order of the classes is also a sacred cow of scheduling. If a student's day begins with math and ends with science, that will often be the case for the entire year. More students have been turned off to a class, not because of the teacher or the subject matter, but because of the time of day that they have the class. We often ask teachers to think back to some of their favorite classes. Then we ask them how many of those classes were right after lunch, or the last period of the day? We will also demonstrate when it may be appropriate to change the order of classes, and how this is accomplished.

WOW, What a Team!

A flexible schedule should allow teams to do three things: change the length of their classes, the order of their classes, and the grouping of the students in their classes. Of course, being able to change the schedule, and actually changing the schedule are two very different things. This is quite a paradigm shift from the traditional schedule, and requires a change in philosophy and practice.

There is a great quote in a great book about sacred cows. In his book, *If it ain't broke . . . BREAK IT!,* author Robert J. Kriegel says, "Sacred cows make the best burgers." We say that it is time for a sacred cow barbecue! We are going to look at the paradigm shift in scheduling (Figure 8–1) that will allow the instructional practices to drive the schedule. The purpose of this chapter is to demonstrate practical examples to help teams gain control of their instructional time. Instead of getting the sands of time kicked in their face, we will show teams how to flex their scheduling muscle. It is time for a shift, and as a great friend and middle level expert, Mary Mantei, says, "Shift happens!"

SCHEDULING PARADIGM SHIFT

INFLEXIBLE TRADITIONAL SCHEDULE		FLEXIBLE BLOCK SCHEDULE
1. Class length locked in (uniform bell schedule)	➡	1. Vary class length as needed (no bells)
2. Class order locked in	➡	2. Vary class order as needed
3. Student groupings locked in	➡	3. Vary student groupings as needed

Figure 8–1. Scheduling paradigm shift, from traditional scheduling practices to flexible scheduling.

One young man's (a seventh grader) appraisal of flexible scheduling demonstrates the positive impact of a flexible schedule. While working with teams at a school during their team conference periods, we happened to be in the hallway during a late afternoon break. The team in this area was experimenting with a rotating schedule (see Figure 8–5), so we stopped the young man to ask him what he thought about it. What he said should be included in all of the research about flexible scheduling.

Randy asked, "What do you think about not always having the same classes at the same time every day?" He replied, "Oh, mister, this is great. Let me tell you!" At this point he was becoming more excited and animated, as only a seventh grader can. He pointed into one of the rooms and continued, "You know Mrs. Jones in there? When I have her in the morning she is seriously mean! I can't even tiptoe past her without getting yelled at! But, in the afternoon after she has had some coffee and she's been fed, she's pretty nice!" Lunch and coffee may not have been the only factors, but that was all the evidence we needed to know that the rotating schedule was working for at least some of the students.

Flexible Scheduling

The following examples demonstrate how to utilize a flexible block schedule. They are adaptable to any block and any team size. For the sake of simplicity, examples are based on the parameters listed in Figure 8–2. The examples demonstrated here can be accomplished by teams of any size, regardless of the number of minutes in the instructional block. This schedule will work with two to eight member teams with teachers teaching from four to seven periods in schedules with six to ten period days.

SCHEDULING PARAMETERS FOR EXAMPLES

A seven-period day with 45-minute periods and five-minute passing time.

A five-person team where each teacher will teach five of the seven periods. The teachers have planning periods 1 & 2, and teach periods 3-7.

Team name: The Manatees

This means the Manatee students are in Exploratories for 95 minutes and with the core team for 245 minutes (including passing time).

Figure 8–2. All of the examples will be based on these parameters.

THE BLOCKS LOOK LIKE:

	EXPLORATORY 95 minutes		CORE 245 minutes				
	1.	2.	3.	4.	5.	6.	7.
1. Jason	PL	PL	MA	MA	MA	MA	MA
2. Paul	PL	PL	SS	SS	SS	SS	SS
3. Sue	PL	PL	LA	LA	LA	LA	LA
4. Shirley	PL	PL	SCI	SCI	SCI	SCI	SCI
5. Jan	PL	PL	PE	PE	PE	PE	PE

The manatees have a total of 245 minutes of instructional and passing time, which is represented by the **CORE** block on the previous page. The students are away from the team for 95 minutes, which is represented by the **EXPLORATORY** block on the previous page. We are not going to discuss how to build a flexible schedule, but rather, how to use one. We will make one technical note here. It is best that the times for exploratory classes always cover consecutive periods.

The exploratory team can also flex their schedule if they have students in two or more period blocks. The core team block should have as many periods together as possible. The best way to accomplish this in our seven period day example, is to have teams off during periods one and two, or three and four, or four and five, or six and seven. This will always give teams two, three, or five period blocks to work with. There are other options, but that is as technical as we want to get for the purposes of this chapter. Now, let's have some fun flexing our block.

```
REMEMBER:
FLEXING YOUR SCHEDULE
REQUIRES
FLEXING YOUR IMAGINATION
```

Changing Class Length ———————————— ■●▲

The following examples give teams a starting point from which to build their scheduling muscle. We encourage adaptations to these examples to fit situations that do not fit the traditional schedule. Begin by changing the length of classes, then change the assessment process with common tests, create remediation and enrichment time, run double length classes, and, finally, give each other additional planning time.

Example One — Give Common Tests

Next Tuesday is the social studies test. Traditionally, the social studies teacher gives the test each period of the day, and the students take the test whenever they happen to have social studies. For some it is first thing in the morning, and for others it is at the end of the day. There are advantages and disadvantages to taking the test each of those times. The worst time of all, however, may be after lunch. Imagine the young man who has been chasing his girlfriend around the cafeteria. She breaks up with him (or decides to go with him), and he has to take the test sweaty and heartbroken, or with hormones peaking. This is not a pretty sight either way.

So, the Manatees will give all of their students the social studies test at the beginning of their block. The teachers can give the test in their rooms, or the team can give the test in a common area such as the cafeteria, auditorium, or any large group instruction area. After the test, the team can proceed with their regular schedule of classes, only with shorter classes. In addition to equity in the assessment process, there are other advantages.

Test days are often non-instructional days for the teacher giving the test. In this example, the teachers run their regular schedule with shorter classes after the test has been given. That means that instead of being a professional test giver all day, the social studies teacher gives the test one time, and then teaches the rest of the day.

Test length is most often dictated by class length. Now test length is not predetermined by how long the periods are. The teacher giving the test may make it as long or as short as is appropriate. Under normal circumstances, I would defy you to give a 35-minute test in a 45-minute period, and do anything very productive with the remaining ten minutes. Now we give the 35-minute test, and put all of those ten minutes segments into instruction.

Figure 8–3 demonstrates how the Manatees could divide the block time after the team administers a 45-minute social studies test. The team will give the test for 45 minutes, and divide the remaining time evenly for their classes. That will give 40 minutes for each of the classes. The team will also decide how much time to give for passing, which will come out of each class. In this example, we will give three minutes to the passing time, to leave 37 minutes for each class.

1	2	45 minutes	3	4	5	6	7
Exploratories & Planning		Social Studies Test	37 min	37 min	37 min	37 min	37 min

245 minutes - 45 minutes = 200 minutes

200 minutes ÷ 5 classes = 40 minutes

40 minutes - 3 minutes passing = 37 minute classes

Figure 8–3. Calculating class length after giving a 45-minute test in a 245-minute instructional block.

Example Two — Extended Instructional Time

In this example, the team will create longer instructional periods. The longer periods will allow the teachers to use a variety of instructional strategies. This is particularly good for labs, learning centers, projects, and other strategies that require more time than the regular class length. Teachers and students also have to prepare for fewer classes each day. Teachers will see each class three times during the week.

In this example, the team will divide their instructional block each day by three instead of five. We will put in five-minute passing times, (one passing will be four minutes because the division does not come out evenly), which will give the teachers 77-minute classes. Figure 8–4 shows how the team will follow their normal pattern, but will only see three of their classes each day. Also notice that the exploratory teachers are running double classes in what is often called an A/B schedule.

Day	Class period / length			
	1	3	4	5
Monday	Exploratory 95 minutes	77 minutes	77 minutes	77 minutes
	2	6	7	3
Tuesday	Exploratory 95 minutes	77 minutes	77 minutes	77 minutes
	1	4	5	6
Wednesday	Exploratory 95 minutes	77 minutes	77 minutes	77 minutes
	2	7	3	4
Thursday	Exploratory 95 minutes	77 minutes	77 minutes	77 minutes
	1	5	6	7
Friday	Exploratory 95 minutes	77 minutes	77 minutes	77 minutes

Figure 8–4. Creating extended classes.

WOW, What a Team!

Example One — Rotating Schedule

A rotating schedule was the strategy that prompted the positive response from the young man in the introduction. An example of a simple rotation follows. Teams can rotate their schedule daily, weekly, monthly, or by the marking period. The idea is that a student is not locked into any particular class happening at the same time of day for the entire year. Figure 8–5 will show the exploratory classes rotating and blocking as well.

Day	Class					
Monday	Exploratory	3	4	5	6	7
Tuesday	Exploratory	4	5	6	7	3
Wednesday	Exploratory	5	6	7	3	4
Thursday	Exploratory	6	7	3	4	5
Friday	Exploratory	7	3	4	5	6

Figure 8–5. A rotating class schedule.

Example Two — A Rotating Drop Schedule

Often teams want to add "special attractions" to their schedule without eliminating any of their regular classes. Some examples would include state assessment review, reading, literature, and other special classes as needed. Other examples could be a time to work on science projects, study skills, group problem solving, or a team play or skit.

The idea is to add the new class into the rotation and drop one class out each day. The teachers will be teaching six classes in their rotation. The sixth class is the new class, which might be a state assessment skills review class. In Figure 8–6, each class will meet five out every six days with one class dropping out of the schedule each day. This schedule demonstrates the benefits of a rotation, and adds an extra class. Here the extra class is represented by the eighth period.

Day	Class						Class Dropped
Monday	Exploratory	3	4	5	6	7	8
Tuesday	Exploratory	4	5	6	7	8	3
Wednesday	Exploratory	5	6	7	8	3	4
Thursday	Exploratory	6	7	8	3	4	5
Friday	Exploratory	7	8	3	4	5	6
Monday	Exploratory	8	3	4	5	6	7
Tuesday	Exploratory	3	4	5	6	7	8

Figure 8–6. A rotating drop schedule.

Change Student Groupings

Cooperative learning groups do not have to end at the classroom door as the students leave. If cooperative learning strategies are used in the four-core classes one day, the chances are that the students will be in four different groups. Change student groupings to meet different instructional needs. To create class lists, suggest that each team write the names of their students on three by five cards, with one student per card. Use the cards to distribute the students, and create new class lists when moving students from class to class.

One team developed an interdisciplinary teaching unit that required the regrouping of their students. Review their use of this scheduling strategy. This team created an interdisciplinary unit around a math lesson.

The math teacher on the team had a teaching unit he called "bid writing." The math teacher created five person cooperative learning groups in each of his classes. He instructed the groups that they were going to become construction companies. The first job was for the group to come up with a name and an ad for their company.

The math teacher explained that the school board had approved each school in the district to build up to three pre-approved decks. The decks would be for students to be able to do class work outside. They might also be used at lunch, weather permitting. The math teacher then handed out three sets of plans for the decks, which were supposedly approved by the school board.

Then the teacher handed out an ordering catalog for a local lumber company. The catalog contained all of the tools and materials these start-up companies would need to build the decks. Each company had to figure an estimated cost for building each deck. The students had to figure in the tools as well as the materials.

The language arts teacher became involved because she was having the students write business letters to go along with their bid sheets. The problem for the language arts teacher was that the students were not grouped in her class the same way they were in math. When she would tell the students to get into their construction companies, she would have part of one company in one class and part of the same company in another class.

The science teacher and social studies teacher became involved as the students studied environmental issues and local history. The local history included the logging industry and a visit to a working mill. The science requirement was that each company includes an environmental policy as a part of their bid. Unfortunately, the students were not grouped in science and social studies like they were in math, so the companies were not always together.

Regrouping the Students

During this unit, it would be beneficial for the students to be scheduled in their classes by their construction companies. That means that the groups assigned in the math classes needed to extend into the other classes. Therefore, the math teacher will take the cards with student's names on them and arrange them by company, from each of his classes. At the Thursday team meeting before the unit begins, the math teacher will lay out the cards on a table in sets organized by construction companies and by periods. The team will pick and choose from the sets of cards to create their classes. When all of the sets of cards have been distributed, the teachers can make up their new class lists for this unit.

The schedules will be posted and the teams will go through them during advisory time the following week. Students will travel from class to class with their construction company. They have different companies in each of their classes so that classes are still mixed. The difference now is that every teacher can give an assignment for a company to work on, and know that the entire company is there.

This team will regroup their students to allow the groups formed in the math classes to extend into the other classes. They also flex their time using the extended learning time example in Figure 8–4. The ultimate in flexing comes in the last two days of this unit. The companies are allowed to make their own schedules. They tell their teachers which teachers they need to see, and for how long. One company may have the bid sheet done, but need to work on their environmental policy. That company may choose to spend the entire day with the science teacher, and in the media center. Each company first reports to the teacher that they begin their block time with, and works with that teacher to coordinate their schedule for the day. This truly empowers the students, and makes them partners in their learning.

Practice Activity ——————————————— ■●▲

Using your instructional block, create a schedule for one of the given examples. Use your beginning and ending time to actually divide the time into the instructional periods you have decided to use. Remember to show the actual passing times so that your team will know when to move their students.

CONCLUSION

Our responsibility as teachers is to deliver the curriculum using a variety of methods and strategies to meet the unique needs and characteristics of the early adolescents. Flexing the schedule is essential to create times that are appropriate for various instructional strategies. Flexible scheduling allows teams to flex their instructional muscle as well.

Chapter 9

Curriculum Development

━━━━━━━━━━━━━━━━━━━━━━━━━━━━━ ■●▲

"One can never consent to creep
when one feels an impulse to soar."
—Helen Keller

Chapter 9

The purpose of this chapter is to present an overview of curriculum coordination. This is an important area in the realm of team teaching. An entire book could be devoted to the subject, but for our purposes the basics and beginning stages of team collaboration in the arena of curriculum will be presented. A general outlook of curriculum coordination is the focus for this section.

The concept of curriculum coordination is frequently referred to as interdisciplinary instruction. This method of teaching reduces fragmented learning. Interdisciplinary instruction promotes coordination among subjects. Teachers look for opportunities to tie in more than one subject during a teaching unit. Students are able to see the connections among the different subjects during interdisciplinary instruction.

COW ■●▲

A method commonly used by a variety of schools is the COW method. COW refers to Curriculum On the Wall. Many teachers have been required to write down their lesson plans weekly, monthly, or even yearly on a matrix for the administration. However, lesson plans written for the team or principal are brief compared to the teacher's lesson plan book, which is often filed and never looked at again. The method described in this chapter will encourage continual discussion of the lesson plans for all team members throughout the year. This is a simple method that requires little time and is well worth the effort invested. The process of mapping the curriculum is easily divided into three phases.

Materials ■●▲

The team will need some poster board, pens or thin markers, and post-it notes. The team will need different color post-it notes for each subject. The poster board will need to be divided by subjects and weeks in the school year. The poster boards will be taped end to end as the year progresses.

Phase One — Build the COW

Teachers fill in the post-it notes after the week is completed. The purpose is to record what has been done, not to plan what is going to be done next week. A sample post-it note is shown in Figure 9–1. In the upper left corner of the post-it note, the number of the week is listed. The content should be in the middle of the post-it note. The content should be in pen or fine point marker and should be only a few words with large print. It is best to state the content simply without educational jargon. The bottom of the post-it note could be the state skills or standards. This should also be in abbreviated notation. It is recommended to complete this task weekly, as monthly is often too broad and requires too much writing on the post-it note. Also, once the team begins to tie in common threads and move post-it notes, it will be obvious that monthly summaries have too much information.

Post-It™ Notes

```
┌─────────────────────────────┐
│ # (of week)                 │
│                             │
│                             │
│          CONTENT            │
│                             │
│        Skills/Standards     │
│                             │
│                             │
└─────────────────────────────┘
```

Figure 9–1. Sample of one Post-It™ note.

Points to Remember

▲ One post-it note per week.

● Complete the post-it note at the end of the week.

▲ Use different color post-it notes for each subject.

● Use poster boards taped end to end.

Phase Two — Connect It ────────────── ■ ● ▲

Phase Two follows Phase One. This is the part where the team stands away from the map and looks at all curriculum areas. It is important during this phase to find connections among subjects. Team members should look for words or phrases that indicate similar skills in different areas. If the math teacher notices that the same skill is taught in a different week during science, then the math teacher should make a copy of the math post-it note and stick it to the science note. It is important to keep the original note in place for future reference. A sample of five weeks is shown in Figure 9–2. The map should be made out of poster board. The electives or exploratory course may be expanded depending on selections offered at specific schools.

Curriculum Mapping "COW"

Week	1	2	3	4	5
Math					
Science					
Social Studies					
Language Arts					
P.E. and Electives					

Figure 9–2. Curriculum on the wall (COW) map
for five weeks.

Phase Three — Develop It ━━━━━━━━━━━━ ■●▲

This is the point where post-it notes have been added to
other post-it notes that have similar skills. Now it is time to
incorporate the connected subjects. The teachers should make
an effort to coordinate the units appropriately to enhance
student learning. Begin small and notice the little common
threads. The science and math teachers may notice a connection
and opt to do a coordinated unit on measurement while the
English and history teacher coordinate a poetry unit. If there is
an area that is relevant to most subjects and a theme emerges,
expand on that theme. There are teams who have outstanding
units based on a theme, such as a Middle Age festival, science
and math fair, career night, etc.

Practice Activity ■●▲

It would be most helpful if post-it notes were utilized for this activity. However, the two squares in Figure 9–3 may be used in lieu of post-it notes. Please remember that it is highly recommended that teams utilize the COW. It is essential to see the curriculum on the wall.

Think of the last week that you taught. Write down on a post-it note the number of the week, the content, and the state standard covered. If you can remember more than the last week, use both post-it notes.

Once you have an idea of how to write out the post-it note(s) and where to place the post-it note(s), introduce the mapping technique to your team. Begin with small steps and only ask team members to write the information from last week on the post-it note. Team members will see that this concept is manageable once they are invited to share three things—the week number, content, and standard.

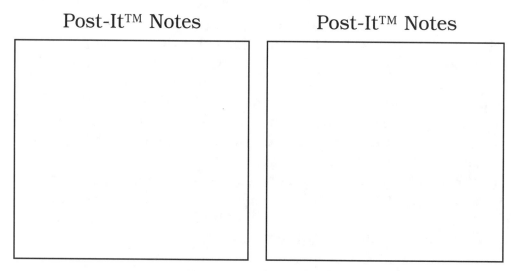

Figure 9–3. Activity squares for content, skill, and week number.

WOW, What a Team!

CONCLUSION

Interdisciplinary instruction is a powerful teaching strategy. The disciplines are integrated together for an enhanced learning experience. A helpful method to begin the process is the COW technique discussed in this chapter. The task of building the maps should be prescheduled on a period per week starting the second or third week of school (see chapter two). Teachers utilize this time to fill in the appropriate information on the post-it notes. Once a team has experience mapping, a fourth phase may be added which incorporates community learning. Phase four requires commitment from all team members to take the unit to a higher level and involve members outside the school.

Chapter 10

Professional Development

■●▲

"Do not believe in anything because you have heard it.
Do not believe in traditions because they have been
handed down for many generations.
Do not believe in anything because it is spoken and
rumored by many.
Do not believe in anything because it is found written
in your religious books.
Do not believe in anything merely on the authority of
your teachers and elders.
But after observation and analysis, when you find that
anything agrees with reason and is conducive to the
good and benefit of one and all, then accept it and
live up to it."

—Buddha

Chapter 10

Continual professional growth is vital for individuals and teams. Professional development can range from coursework to sharing information. The team environment is designed to encourage communication and collaboration. The sharing process promotes learning and growth for students and teachers. For example, each time a team member attends a workshop or conference, time should be put on the agenda to discuss new ideas acquired from their experience.

An activity that encourages active involvement, knowledge of current events and reading, and promotes discussion and sharing information is the Reading Club. Reading Club meetings should be prescheduled monthly meetings. For example, one team has designated the first team meeting of each month as their Reading Club meeting. This gives each team member an entire month to read the required information.

Reading Club

The team leader or professional development person on the team selects a book or an article. The resource needs to be a current selection in the field. Suggestions for the title may be given to the team leader.

Each team member has the same assignment to complete by the date determined by the team. The task is to read the required reading material. It is feasible to assign an article for members to read. If a book is selected for the reading, the first chapter would be the assignment for the next Reading Club meeting.

WOW, What a Team!

Team members bring the chapter, book, or article to the discussion meeting. The team leader or professional development person on the team establishes an assessment sheet for the meeting. The entire time is devoted to discussion of the material and application to the team.

Example

A popular resource utilized by many in education and business is *The 7 Habits of Highly Effective People* by Stephen R. Covey (Fireside Publishing, 1990). The habits are listed below.

Habit 1   Be Proactive / *Principles of Personal Vision*

Habit 2   Begin with the End in Mind / *Principles of Personal Leadership*

Habit 3   Put First Things First / *Principles of Personal Management*

Habit 4   Think Win/Win / *Principles of Interpersonal Leadership*

Habit 5   Seek 1st to Understand, then to be Understood / *Principles of Empathic Communication*

Habit 6   Synergize / *Principles of Creative Cooperation*

Habit 7   Sharpen the Saw / *Principles of Balanced Self-Renewal*

The assignment for the team in this example would be to read the first chapter of *The 7 Habits of Highly Effective People.* Team members would read the chapter and reflect on themselves. Team members would need to bring their books to the Reading Club meeting. The assessment sheet would determine the format of the meeting. A sample assessment sheet is shown on page 130.

Date ___ / ___ / ___

Assessment of
The 7 Habits of Highly Effective People

Please take ten minutes to read the questions and jot some responses down. Items 1–8 will be discussed as a team and items 9–10 will be for personal reflection.

1. What is the main idea of this chapter?

2. What does "Be Proactive" mean to you?

3. Is this team proactive?

4. Do you need to be proactive to be effective? Why or why not?

5. How does this chapter relate to education?

6. How does this chapter relate to our school?

7. How does this chapter relate to our team?

8. How would you rate this chapter?

Personal Reflection

9. Are you proactive?

10. How does this chapter relate to you?

Practice Activity ━━━━━━━━━━━━━━━━━━━━ ■●▲

Some sources are listed below to use with this chapter. You may choose to use an article you have recently read or a chapter from a book. There are many resources available for growth. Select one that is enjoyable for your team. Educational tips are available online at www.edugator.com if you prefer to download information. An outstanding book on change that may prove advantageous is *Who Moved My Cheese?* by Spencer Johnson (Putnam Publishing Group, 1998). For more information regarding this resource, connect to www.whomovedmycheese.com. Please take a few moments to read one of the following articles or books (or one of your choice) and develop a Reading Club assessment sheet for the source. A blank form is provided on page 132.

Managing Your Mind: What Are You Telling Yourself?
Christopher Neck and Annette Barnard
Educational Leadership v53 n 6 March 1996

To Be Intelligent
John Abbott
Educational Leadership v54 n6 March 1997

The Good Mentor
James B. Rowley
Educational Leadership v56 n8 May 1999

What makes a High-Achieving Middle School?
Lauren Kanthak
Education Digest v61 n7 March 1996

Blanchard, K., & Johnson, S. (1983). *The One Minute Manager.* New York: Berkley Books.

Kouzes, J.M., & Posner, B. (1996). *The Leadership Challenge: How to get extraordinary things done in organizations, ed. 2.* San Francisco: Jossey-Bass.

Senge, P.M. (1990) *The Fifth Discipline: The art and practice of the learning organization.* New York: Doubleday.

Reading Club Assessment

Date ___ / ___ / ___
Title of source _____
Author _____

1. _____

   _____

2. _____

   _____

3. _____

   _____

4. _____

   _____

5. _____

   _____

6. _____

   _____

7. _____

   _____

8. _____

   _____

9. _____

   _____

10. _____

   _____

WOW, What a Team!

CONCLUSION

Reading Club time may be used to share information gathered at a recently attended conference or workshop. Reading Club time may also be used to invite a guest speaker to address the team on a topic of high interest to team members. Many teams report that the Reading Club time is their favorite team meeting time. Hopefully, this staff development exercise will be productive and beneficial for your team. Growth and change is not an easy process, but often leads to remarkable results. Good luck!

Chapter 11

Assessing
Team Success

■●▲

"Success isn't permanent and failure isn't fatal."
—Mike Ditka

Chapter 11

The Japanese word *Kaizen* is the term used to mean *continuous improvement*. It is the relentless quest for a better way and higher quality. Kaizen is the daily pursuit of perfection. To practice Kaizen, a person or group must already be very skilled. Kaizen does not mean that what you are doing now is bad. In fact, what your are doing is very good, and Kaizen is the search for a way to make the good even better. Kaizen also implies that the person or group will be open to changes that may lead to higher performance.

Teams need a process for reviewing and assessing their progress in order to practice Kaizen. Teams need to celebrate their successes to maintain a high level of performance, and make corrections as needed to continue to grow and improve. The assessment process should be personal to each team, reflecting their vision of success.

This chapter will involve taking a personal, and then a cumulative look at what makes for successful teaming. It is helpful to have some sort of a checklist to use for evaluating performance. In lieu of using some generic and sterile assessment instrument, we will help you to generate an instrument for assessing teaming in your school. This instrument will be built around your (and your teammates', if possible) vision of successful teaming.

In this chapter, standards for great teaming will be developed. You will break down a team meeting to determine what should and what should not be happening during productive team meetings. To maximize the impact of teaming, teams should be meeting daily in a schedule that allows for a team planning period and an individual planning period. Unfortunately, teachers in some schools only have one period to use as both the team and the individual planning period. In both situations it is important that teams have an assessment process.

How often teams meet should be a site-based decision with all teams meeting for approximately the same amount of time each week. In other words, there never should be an argument on a team about how many days a week they should meet. The decision regarding how many days a week teams will meet should be made as a school. The teams can then plan accordingly.

Effective teams have regular observation meetings whether they meet as a team one day a week or daily. Observation meetings are ones where the team reviews its progress. Team members make observations regarding team performance, and make suggestions for improvement. It is a time to renew spirits and refocus. Teams that are meeting daily could have an observation meeting monthly. Teams that meet less often may have observation meetings once every marking period or semester.

The checklist that is generated during this chapter will be the instrument teams will use during observation meetings. Teammates will go through the checklist discussing any areas where any team member feels there is a need for improvement. It is also important for a team to make note of accomplishments, and celebrate their successes.

Practice Activity

Brainstorm lists of descriptors for effective teaming and productive team meetings. Then, make the lists into a checklist for use in observation meetings.

The lists are generated in three areas according to the scenarios described in Part One, Part Two, and Part Three. If at all possible have your teammates do the activity as well, and then combine your lists. In fact, this is a great all-staff activity. It is important that each of the lists be as comprehensive as possible. Therefore, take the time to go into as much detail as possible. Consider the following scenarios and take about fifteen minutes to complete the task of listing the descriptors called for in each part.

Part One

Imagine that you are giving us a tour of your building. As we walk around, we pass by a room where a team meeting is taking place. You get called away for a while. As we stand outside waiting for you to return, we can hear what they are saying in the meeting, but we cannot see into the room. After listening for a while, you return, and we say to you "WOW, what a team! They really work well together, don't they?"

Or, imagine that the intercom system has been turned on in a room where a team meeting is in progress. Of course, being of a very curious nature, we listen to the meeting. As we listen, what we hear indicates to us that there is a great team meeting going on with an awesome team.

Now, suppose we are going to create a cassette tape of several team meetings to train new teachers on how to work on a team. Think about the auditory cues you would expect to hear which indicate that we are hearing very productive teams. It may help to close your eyes as you think of the sounds. Try to think about the subtle sounds, and remember that we will listen to several team meetings. We also want you to think about what sounds you would *not* hear in a productive team meeting.

Make a list of what would and would not be heard while listening to productive teams conduct meetings. Break down any broad areas such as "positive climate", then list what makes for a positive climate. Figure 11–1 demonstrates some examples of the categories and indicators that might be included.

SOUNDS OF PRODUCTIVE TEAMS

1. Positive Climate
   A. Positive comments
   B. Sound of food
   C. Laughter
2. Productive Work
   A. On task
   B. Following an agenda
   C. Materials being used

3. Everyone Participating
   A. Everyone's voice
   B. Paraphrasing
   C. Consensus
4. Other Participants
   A. Social worker
   B. Parent
   C. Student

**SOUNDS YOU SHOULD NOT HEAR
DURING TEAM MEETINGS**

1. Put-downs

2. Off task discussion

3. Refusal to participate

Figure 11–1. Examples of sounds that should and should not be a part of productive team meetings.

Part Two

Imagine that as we tour the building, we go past some windows that look into a team area. We see a team meeting going on, but cannot hear a word they are saying. We watch for quite a while, seeing, but not hearing, as they run their meeting. Again, after watching for a while, we are very impressed with what we see. It is very apparent that this is also a WOW team having a great team meeting.

Suppose we videotape several model team meetings for a training program for teaming. When we play the videos back we realize that we forgot to turn on the audio. However, this is okay because these videos really show what team meetings should look like.

Of course, sometimes it is what we do not see as well as what we do see that indicate great collaboration and performance. List everything one would "see" and then what one would not "see" that indicate these are productive team meetings. Figure 11–2 lists examples of categories and indicators that might be included.

WOW, What a Team!

SIGHTS OF PRODUCTIVE TEAMS

1. Positive Body Language
   A. Smiles
   B. Leaning forward
   C. Hand motions
2. Positive Climate
   A. Round table
   B. Decorations
   C. Food

3. Participation
   A. All present
   B. Materials ready
   C. Everyone talks
4. Other Participants
   A. Principal
   B. Counselor
   C. Student

THINGS YOU SHOULD NOT SEE DURING A TEAM MEETING

1. Grading papers

2. People arriving late

3. Team members not in attendance

4. Angry gestures

Figure 11–2. Examples of things that should and should not be seen during team meetings.

Part Three

Think about a particular group or team that you may have been a part of that was productive and that you really enjoyed. It might be a sports team, a civic group, a church group, a bowling team, etc. What made being a part of that team or group enjoyable? What did it feel like to be a member of that team or group?

List the feelings that come with being a member of a productive team. Why was working with the group enjoyable? What does it feel like to enjoy working with and being a member of a team or group? At the same time, think about groups, teams, or classes that were not enjoyable. Why was that a negative experience? What would have made it better? List those feelings as well. Figure 11–3 lists examples of categories and indicators that might be included on your list.

WHAT BEING ON A GREAT TEAM FEELS LIKE

1. Supportive
   A. Members help each other
   B. Never put down
   C. Share tasks
2. Productive
   A. Common goals
   B. There is a product
   C. Successful
3. Trust
   A. Able to take risks
   B. Confidentiality
   C. Esprit de Corps
4. Fun
   A. Celebrate successes
   B. Recognition
   C. Acceptance

REASONS TO NOT LIKE BEING ON A TEAM

1. Dread attending
2. Cannot trust team members
3. Back stabbing
4. Arguing
5. Differences in philosophy
6. Nothing gets done

Figure 11–3. Examples of feelings that should and should not be part of being a member of a team.

Culminating Activity ─────────────────── ■●▲

Finally, put the lists created and developed in this chapter into a checklist format. Select items from both the positive and negative lists. Be as comprehensive as possible, but some items may have to be eliminated due to duplication, etc. Put a line in front of each descriptor that remains in the list to create the checklist format.

The final checklist will have the criteria for what a team should look like, sound like, and feel like. You and your teammates can then go down the checklist during observation meetings. The lists will prompt discussion as you and your teammates review and reflect on each item. Your three lists may begin like these:

Great teaming sounds like:
___ Everyone is participating
___ They stay on task
___ There is laughter
___ Paraphrasing
___ No put-downs

Great teaming looks like:
___ Smiles
___ Food on the table
___ Materials ready
___ Eye contact
___ No grading papers

Great teaming feels like:
___ Common goals
___ Productive
___ Safe to take a risk
___ Respect confidentiality
___ Trust

CONCLUSION

Teams need to continually review and reflect in regard to their performance. To do this, teams should schedule regular Observation meetings to discuss how the team is working. This should happen at least once a semester. At Observation meetings, teams should go over their personal checklist. Does our team look like our list says? Does our team sound like our list says it should? Does our team feel like our checklist says it should? If not, why?

For example, one line of an effective team's checklist may have "No one is grading papers." Well, if team members have been grading papers in meetings, it will come out here without one team member having to confront another. In this way, the checklist can be both diagnostic and prescriptive. Observation meetings give the team the opportunity to discuss team-meeting issues, celebrate successes, review team goals, and refocus.

We have worked with many teams as administrators and consultants. Some teams will need more support than others. Randy relates the following story about one of his teams from his experiences as a middle school principal. The names have been left out to protect the innocent and the not-so-innocent.

IT'S ALL YOUR FAULT

My secretary called me one day to go to the planning room for one of my teams. She said I should get to the planning room NOW! My secretary was usually unflappable, and if she ever raised her voice at all, it usually meant that she had also already called 911! So, I hurried to the room to see what was going on.

As I got to the door, I noticed that one of the teachers on the team was standing in the doorway facing in toward the room. I thought that she was going into the room, and stepped in behind her to follow her in. She had actually been leaving but had turned suddenly to face back into the room. As I stepped up behind her, she took the very large textbook in her right hand and threw it onto the table where the other teachers were sitting. As she swung her arm back to make the throw, she almost hit me in the nose with the book. I was quick enough to dodge the book, but it made a huge sound as it slammed onto the table, and papers went flying everywhere.

As the book slammed onto the surface of the table, she called one of the other teachers in the room a very naughty name in a fairly loud voice. I was stepping in behind her to follow her into the room when she suddenly spun around to storm out of the room. It became quickly obvious that she had not seen me behind her, because she ran into me trying to get out. I tried to get out of her way, but we met basically chest to chest much the way athletes do when celebrating, only she was not celebrating.

I took about a half step back to get out of harm's way, but she stepped right toward me and put the index finger of her right hand squarely into the middle of my forehead. Then, with her finger against my forehead, and in the same loud voice she yelled, "AND IT'S YOUR FAULT!" Then she took off down the hallway. Well, being the highly trained and skilled professional administrator that I am, I realized that there was a problem.

This team had come to be Webster's definition for a dysfunctional team. In fact, I think their picture still appears in the dictionary. The easiest and most obvious solution for this team was to break it up and reconfigure the teams at that grade level. But then we would not have addressed the issues, and they would have shown up again on the new teams. While working with this team, we did the activity explored in this chapter to redefine what they were to be doing as a team. I also did some team-building activities with the team, and we worked through the problems.

The team began to hold monthly observation meetings, and they began to work together. I believe that teams that face adversity together and survive become the best teams. For this particular team, that certainly proved to be true. They were my first team to do Thumbs Meetings (chapter five), to truly integrate their curriculums (chapter nine), and to take on student-led conferences. This team had the most difficult time as we began the teaming process. As I think about this team, I am constantly reminded that teaming is a process, and not an event.

The activity in this chapter helped that team focus on the technical aspects of teaming, and not on the personalities involved. If this team had remained focused on the personalities involved, someone would probably be doing jail time. Instead, they began to focus on what great teams should look like, sound like, and feel like. They focused on student achievement, and not personal issues. By the way, I am sure you are curious about what caused the original argument. The team was discussing their discipline policy, and the volatile topic was gum chewing. This was several years ago, and the team mentioned above is still together. When that finger was in my forehead, I wasn't so optimistic.

WOW, What a Team!

Chapter 12

Team Goals

■●▲

"Whatever the mind can conceive and believe,
it can achieve."
—*Napoleon Hill*

Chapter 12

Effective teams establish goals that are meaningful, clearly stated, and easily measured. Meaningful goals will reflect the school's goals and will impact student performance.

Goal statements are either affective or cognitive, and effective teams will establish goals in each area. Affective goals may include the advisory program, attendance, team identity, and so on. Affective goals generally deal with the students as persons. Cognitive goals may include curriculum mapping, developing interdisciplinary units, shared assessment, instructional strategies, and so on. Cognitive goals deal with the academic program, and the academic performance of the students. Some goals incorporate both, like service learning.

Team Goals

Read the following information about team goals. The activity for this chapter will be to write sample goals that would be appropriate for your team in your school.

For goals to be measurable, they must have specific criteria that can be documented. An affective goal may be a certain percent of decrease in discipline referrals from a team. With access to the discipline data from last year, documenting this goal is easy, and success will have a direct correlation to overall student success.

A cognitive goal may be to raise the overall grade point average for the team, or the average scores on the state assessment test, or reduce the number of failures. All of these are measurable, and will document team success.

WOW, What a Team!

Whether affective, cognitive, or a combination, goals are usually measured as some predetermined percent gain in a positive indicator, or a percent decrease in a negative indicator. Goals should challenge the teachers and students on a team, but they should be realistic. It is all right to surpass goals, but it is often depressing not to reach them. So, set goals high, but be sure they are attainable.

Teams may try to attain a certain percent of increase in areas such as mentors, business partnerships, parental involvement, test scores, student attendance, and student recognition. Teams may also try to attain a certain percent decrease in areas such as discipline referrals, tardiness to classes or to school, the number of missed or late assignments, or the number of failures. Figure 12-1 contains specific examples of both goal types.

GOAL EXAMPLES

▲ Increase student performance on the math portion of the state assessment test by at least 10%.

● Decrease student discipline referrals by at least 15%.

▲ Increase parent participation at parent conferences by at least 20%.

● Decrease tardiness to class by at least 15%.

▲ Increase student participation in the community service project by at least 10%.

Figure 12–1. Goal examples demonstrating a percent of increase or decrease in various areas.

With each goal statement, teams then need to list strategies for accomplishing the goal (Figure 12–2). These strategies should be discussed regularly to assess and adjust as needed. Strategy statements should only include strategies within the control of the team. For example, a strategy of increasing the team budget may be something the team really has no control over. However, a strategy that includes how to spend the team's budget is within the control of the team.

Teams should also include timelines indicating when or how often each strategy is to happen as they discuss their strategies. For example, one team established a goal of making five positive phone calls home per teacher per week. One strategy to accomplish this was to dedicate one period every week on Mondays to decide which students would receive positive phone calls, and which teacher would make the calls. Another strategy was to start a separate calling log to keep track of the calls, which they reviewed monthly to keep track of the calls they were making.

STRATEGY EXAMPLES

▲ Create an extra period weekly on a rotation for math assessment review.

● Have a team math competition once per marking period.

▲ Begin having Thumbs Up meetings every two weeks.

● Use advisory activities every Monday to teach respect and reduce discipline referrals.

▲ Create a positive rewards program to recognize students "caught" doing a good deed. Cards will be given to students any time a teacher "catches" them doing a good deed, and there will be a recognition assembly every Friday during team time.

● Start an "Acts of Random Kindness" program. Students will design the program as an advisory activity during the first two weeks of school. The program will be ongoing for the school year, and reviewed each marking period.

▲ Have a motivational kick-off assembly for the community service project during the first parent conferences of the school year.

Figure 12–2. Examples of strategies that include the timeline for implementation of the strategy.

Write three sample goals and share why those goals would be appropriate for your team. If you are a member of a team, this would be best done as a team activity. Make sure that you have a copy of the school goals so that you can be sure your team goals complement the school goals. Be sure to include strategies for the accomplishment of the goal. With each strategy, be sure to include the timeline for the strategy.

Example

The Land Shark team will decrease the number of late assignments by at least 15%.

<u>Strategies will include:</u>

1. Developing a late assignment policy that will be implemented by all of the teachers on the team.
    A. The late assignment policy will be developed during pre-school workdays.
    B. The late assignment policy will be introduced to the parents in the first newsletter, and at the first open house of the school year.
    C. The team will have a motivational opening team meeting with all of the students on the first day of school. The new policy will be introduced during the team meeting.
    D. The policy will apply to all assignments beginning the second week of school.

2. Create a homework buddy system for students to help each other remember and complete assignments.
   A. Students will be assigned homework buddies during the first week of school as a part of their advisory group.
   B. Advisory groups will come together at the end of the school day for 10 minutes for homework buddies to get together.
   C. Homework buddies will call their buddy in the event of absences to inform their buddy of homework assignments.
   D. Homework buddies will be encouraged to work cooperatively, with training during Advisory time.

3. Flex the schedule to create a time to meet with students at the end of the day. During this time remind students about homework assignments; give time for homework buddies to meet, and make sure students are taking home the appropriate materials. This will be for ten minutes each day for the initial phase, and then the team will evaluate the process.

4. Create a weekly team calendar with the assignments for the week on it to be given to students every Monday. The team will finalize the calendar during the first three periods of team time every Friday. The back of the calendar will be the student's pass sheet. Teachers will use the calendar for passes to the bathroom, locker, etc. to help ensure that students keep their calendars with them.

5. Make late assignments part of the academic criteria for Thumbs Up meetings and earning a Thumbs Up certificate. Thumbs Up meetings will occur every two weeks (see chapter five).

CONCLUSION

One of the most important things for teams to do is set goals. Goal discussion will force teams to establish priorities, while the discussion of strategies will provide direction for the team. Students should be actively involved in the strategies for achieving goals and in the documentation of goal attainment. For example, they can be involved in counting data and keeping charts.

Teams should assess goals on a regular basis. Discussion of goals should be a part of every Observation meeting and a part of other meetings as set up by the team. While goals remain constant, strategies should be adjusted, or new strategies added as needed. Many teams establish goals, but only the WOW teams follow through.

One team set a goal to have no referrals to the office for classroom discipline. One strategy they were going to implement was from the book *Positive Discipline in the Classroom* by Jane Nelson (Prima Publishing, 2000). The team went to a training program, and worked together to implement a positive discipline program within their team. They worked very hard early in the school year to get their students trained. They even received criticism from fellow staff for "doing administrator work" in dealing with their own discipline.

In a relatively short time, however, they had their kids following the program. They went to the administrator a couple of times to see if she would make "house calls" to help with some of the tougher discipline issues. She told them she would be happy to make "house calls." and that we would not count those as office referrals. They did make it all year without an office referral for classroom discipline. As they became more empowered, they found that the time they previously used to take to write referrals was now becoming instructional time, which also helped to reduce the amount of discipline.

WOW, What a Team!

A different team started a "Random Acts of Kindness" program as a strategy for an affective goal of getting students involved in a community service project, which called for improving the school climate. As the students began to do their random acts of kindness, what they soon discovered was that people often reciprocated in kind. One act of kindness often ended up in several acts of kindness.

It was really fun to watch the staff. The teachers on this team decided that they needed to model acts of kindness for the students. The team knew that the exploratory teachers were planning for a field day that was coming up soon. They volunteered to keep their students during the exploratory classes and do a team activity with them to give the exploratory teachers two extra planning periods on that day. The exploratory teachers were so impressed that they cooked breakfast for the staff on the next professional development day. One of the eighth grade teams was so impressed by the breakfast that they started putting candy in the teachers' boxes one day a week. We could not list all of the things that the staff thought of to do for each other. The acts of kindness done by that team of teachers and their students started a chain reaction that had a tremendous impact on the school climate.

FINAL THOUGHTS ON A WOW TEAM . . .

An interdisciplinary teaching team is made up of a common group of teachers with a common group of students for a common part of the day. The key word here is common. The teachers on a team have to learn to share students, curriculums, space, and time. This requires a high level of collaboration, along with a great deal of patience and a wonderful sense of humor. The purpose of this book has been to help teachers put WOW into their teams by providing practical strategies that will enhance their efforts. Exemplary middle schools have WOW teams that are masters at collaboration. The learning environments that WOW teams create promote peak performance.

WOW teams become productive and make the most of their team time by committing themselves to training, preparation, and synergy. It is important to remember that becoming a WOW team is a process and not an event. WOW teams are the ones that work constantly to improve. They are always open to finding new and better ways to meet the needs of all of their students. The chapters in this book were presented to illustrate ways that WOW teams have created high-impact team performance. Hopefully, your team will be able to apply some or all of the strategies shared here. Good luck to you and your WOW team!

References and Suggested Readings

Atwell, N. (1998). *In the Middle, ed. 2.* Boynton/Cook Publishers.

Bourman, E. & Bourman, N. (1996). *Effective Small Group Communication, ed. 6.* Edina, Minn. Burgess Publishing.

Chang, R. Y. (1994). *Building a dynamic team.* Irvine, CA: Jossey-Bass.

Clark, J. *Involving parents in the middle school.* Teaching PreK-8, 27(3), 52-53.

Conti-D'Antonio, M., Bertrando, R. & Eisenberger, J. (1998). *Supporting Students With Learning Needs In The Block.* Eye On Education

Connors, N. *If You Don't Feed the Teachers They Eat the Students!* (2000). Nashville, TN. Incentive Publications, Inc.

Covey, S. *The 7 Habits of Highly Effective People.* New York; Fireside Publishing, 1990.

Erb, T. & Doda, N. (1989). *Team organization: Promise, Practices, and Possibilities.* Washington, D.C.: NEA.

Fertman, C., White, L., & White, J. *Service Learning in the Middle School: Building a Culture of Service.* (1996). NMSA.

Fisher, A. (1991). *Strategies for Building Self-Esteem in Gifted Students.* Challenge. Good Apple, Issue 47

Flowers, N., Mertens, S. B., & Mulhall P. F. (2000). *What makes interdisciplinary team effective?* Middle School Journal, 31(4), 53-56.

Forte, I. & Schurr, S. *The Definitive Middle School Guide: A Handbook for Success.* (1993). Nashville, TN. Incentive Publications.

Graves, D. (1996) *Parent meetings: are you ready?* Instructor May-June v105 n8 p42 (2)

Johnson, S. *Who Moved My Cheese?.* (1998). New York: Putnam Publishing Group.

Kain, D. (1993). *Helping teams succeed: an essay review of groups that work (and those that don't): Creating conditions for effective teamwork.* Middle School Journal, 24(4), 25-31.

Kayser, T.A. *Building Team power.* (1994). New York: Irwin Professional Publishers.

Kellough, R., & Kellough, N. *Middle School Teaching: A Guide to Methods and Resources.* (1998). Prentice Hall.

Lounsbury, J. *Connecting the Curriculum Through Interdisciplinary Instruction.* (1992). NMSA

Merenbloom, E. *The team process in the middle school: A handbook for teachers, ed. 3.* (1991). Columbus, OH: NMSA.

Nelson, Jane. *Positive Discipline in the Classroom. 3rd ed.* (2000). New York. Prima Publishing.

Power, B. (1999). *Strengthen your parent connection. Using newsletters to build harmonious parent-teacher relationships.* Instructor Oct v109 i3 p30 (2)

Rose, M. (1998). *Recommended reading for tips on conferences. Handle with care: the difficult parent-teacher conference.* Instructor, Oct 1998 v108 n3 p92 (3)

Rottier, J. *Implementing and Improving Teaming: A Handbook for Middle Level Leaders.* (1996). Columbus, OH. National Middle School Association.

Scearce, Carol *100 Ways to Build Teams.* (1993). Palantine, IL. IRI/Skylight Publishing.

Smith, H. (1991). *Guide teaming development.* Middle School Journal, 22(5), 21-23.

Williams, B. *More than 50 ways to build team consensus.* (1993). Praline, IN. IRI/Skylight.

Websites

www.edugator.com
    This website focuses on middle level education. There is a section designated to educational tips for teachers. Educators are encouraged to learn and share ideas.

www.nmsa.org
    The official site of the National Middle School Association.

www.webed.com
    An online education company dedicated to providing professions with the opportunity to earn professional development credit through Internet-based courses.